GOD BLESS AMERICA

God's Vision, Or Ours?

GOD BLESS AMERICA

God's Vision, Or Ours

Fr. Bill McCarthy, MSA

Queenship

PUBLISHING COMPANY
P.O. Box 220 • Goleta, CA 93116
(800) 647-9882 • (805) 692-0043 • Fax: (805) 967-5133

Without God's vision, people perish.
cf. Proverbs 29:18

Library of Congress Number # 2002095726

Published by:
Queenship Publishing
P.O. Box 220
Goleta, CA 93116
(800) 647-9882 • (805) 692-0043 • Fax: (805) 967-5133
www.queenship.org

Printed in the United States of America

ISBN: 1-57918-225-9

Contents

Preamble

I love my God and I love my country. But somewhere between the founding of our nation and 1962, there was a radical disconnect. Our country has belied its highest ideals which were based upon the natural law and the Scriptures. In section one, we will take a look at a nation born. In section two, we will explore a nation in decay. In Section 3, we will lay out strategies for a nation to be born again.

"If my people who are called by my name will humble themselves and pray and seek my face and turn from their wicked ways, then will I hear from heaven and will forgive their sin and will heal their nation" (2 Chron 7:14)

Twin Towers

When terrorists attacked the twin towers, our people rose in a tremendous display of prayer and patriotism. However, a new and more deadly terrorism was underway. We were no longer God-centered, life-centered, family-centered, decency-centered. Our media was predominately biased, as Bernie Goldberg said in his best-selling book, *Bias*,—a book which clearly exposes the American media as anti-God, anti-Christian, anti-Catholic, anti-family, anti-life, and anti-American. George Washington pointed out that anyone who would attack the twin pillars of America—religion and morality—could not possibly be a loyal patriot.

Elections 2002

The New York Times had a front page article right after the recent elections (Nov. ' 02) that bemoaned the fact that neither major party had a real vision for America. For without God's vision, people perish. Almost no politician raised real issue affecting our country: That we are in so many ways no longer really a nation under God; that secular humanism and New Age thinking affects millions and millions of our fellow citizens; that half the country no longer honors the sanctity of human life; that promiscuity, di-

vorce, obscenity, and violence are "mainstream"; that over 90 percent of our youth are sexually exploited and abused in one way or
another before they reach the age of 18; that families are breaking
down at a catastrophic speed; that younger and younger children
are being vulgarized; that our public schools are in a state of moral
meltdown; that SAT scores in general are down more than 100
points; that socially-transmitted diseases are rampant, and that our
media is increasingly more pagan, biased, pornographic, and dis-
honest.

The End of a Dream

The God-given American dream in many ways is coming to an
end. Godless and humanistic ideas are ruining our nation. If this
nation or any nation so conceived and so dedicated is to long endure, we have to return to the God-given vision of America.

The Dirty Dozen

Please read the 12 principles that made America great and then
compare them to the 12 principles that are leading our country to
ruin. Then ask yourself honestly, which America is better—the
America that existed from 1776 to 1962 as a nation under God
wherein pornography, abortion, public obscenity were outlawed,
where each pubic school child said the *Our Father* publicly and
learned the Ten Commandments, where you had prayer and moral
formation in every classroom, where a minister, priest of rabbi said
the invocation at every graduation, where every youngster had a
dress code, and where the biggest problem were chewing gum, tar-
diness, and an occasional truancy. . . or, this new liberal America
that separates God from state and in so doing separated moral teaching from education, where 50 percent of the student body in most
public high schools never graduate, where pregnancy, social disease, drugs, alcohol, and obscenity are affecting the highest per-
centage of our children.

Which Way to Go

Any honest reading of this book will make it very obvious which way we are to go for the preservation of our nation and salvation of our children. The choice is clear. If we follow, once again, God's principles, we will prosper. If we do not, we will continue to decay from within.

This is the real question of 'choice'—revival or ruin, God or chaos, with Him or without Him, decency of profanity, dignity of abuse, a culture of life of a culture of death, up or down.

Section I - A Nation Born

1
September 11th and Its Aftermath

A Day of Infamy

Hardly any American fails to remember where they were on the fateful morning of September 11, 2001 — a day that, along with December 7, 1941, will go down in history as a day of infamy. America was struck by terrorism and shock waves reverberated throughout our country.

Who Caused This?

Some people think that in some way God caused this. Some readings of the Old Testament, particularly the earlier books, could lead us in this direction. But, as we read on, our image of God grows clearer and becomes deeper still as we hear Jesus say to Phillip, "Have I been with you for so long, and yet you do not know Me? He who has seen me has seen the Father" (Jn 14:9) We, then, come to the question, "Did God cause this catastrophe or any other disaster?" St. Augustine answers the question by saying, "God does not do evil, but does cause that evil should not become the worse" (Soliloquies, 2).

God Was With Us

Almost everybody realizes that, as horrendous as the devastation was, it could have been much worse. As many as 50,000 people could have died if it had happened just an hour later, or if the buildings had fallen over sideways, or if the normal flow of tourism had taken place. Obviously, it would have been terrible enough if just one person had died, but God prevented the evil from becoming worse.

Many Saved By Grace

The twin towers had 40,000 people working in them, and, by the grace of God, most of them got out safely. There were many

1

firefighters, police officers and emergency workers who did manage to survive. One firefighter miraculously rode an elevator down the collapsing building from the 84th floor and survived with two broken legs. Stories of heroism and miraculous escapes have now multiplied, as have stories of people who were prevented from being in the buildings by some providential cause. Yes, "God does not do evil, but does cause that evil should not become the worse."

Good From Evil

It can also be truly said that God causes good to come out of evil. The worst thing that ever happened on this planet earth was that mankind, through our sins, crucified the very Son of God. What, then, is the best thing that ever happened? And the answer is that Jesus died on the cross not only to redeem us from our sins but to save us eternally in heaven. The worst became the best.

St. Thomas Aquinas

St. Thomas Aquinas wisely said that most people who believe in God do so because of the problem of evil. Most of the people who do not believe in God reject Him because of the problem of evil. Faith and lack of faith flow out of our vision of evil. Rain, for example, can cause floods, but also helps the growth of all plants. Volcanic eruptions cause fearful damage to the surrounding areas but bring about beneficial atmospheric changes around the earth.

Answers in Purgatory

The problem of good and evil remains a great mystery. How can a totally good God allow all this evil? We get some insights through the Scriptures. But eventually, we will see the total picture when we get to purgatory — because in heaven, there will be no more questions. The ultimate answer, of course, lies in free will.

A Perfect World

God could have created a perfectly-orchestrated world, a world that would have been completely predetermined even as to man. Like the stars, the rocks, the plants, and much of the animal world, everything would be in perfect union with the absolute will of God.

And even man could be computerized to be perfect. We would eat perfectly, run perfectly, and speak perfectly. But we would be completely incapable of love.

God Is Love

Because God is love, He wanted to make it possible for all persons to be made into His image and likeness. And so He had to give them the freedom of choice to love and obey Him — or not to love and obey Him. Without freedom, there can be no love. Because God is love and prizes love so much, He risked all the evil in the world to get from us the little love we give Him.

A Human Example

We would do the same. If a person had a choice of a computerized, bionic spouse who would react perfectly to our push buttons, or a real live human being (even with all their faults and failings), everyone of us knows intuitively that we would choose not the machine but the person. Why? Because that person is endowed with intellect and will. Thus, only the person would be capable of knowing and loving us. So it is with God.

2
A Blessing and a Curse:
A Promise and a Hope for Our Times

God Is Love

God is love diffusive of itself Who calls forth love on the part of His children. God is simply love — truest love, most respectful love. From God comes only blessings, graces, gifts and life more abundantly. We, on our part, can either receive or reject His love and blessings. If we choose, of our own free will, to accept His blessings, we are blessed indeed. We receive faith and hope, life and love, joy and happiness, and eventually eternal life.

Curses

If we say 'no', that is, if we reject His blessings, we are cursed to live with the results of such rebellion and sin. Rejected blessings, therefore, from our point of view, are our curses. Curses are the lack of God's graces and blessings.

Simply Love
From God's point of view, God, if you will, blesses and curses people by doing the same thing. He gives everyone what they want. Or, more correctly, He is always giving what is good and allows His children to say either yes or no. If we say yes, it will be a blessing. If we say no, we curse ourselves.

A Blessing or a Curse
"See, I'm setting before you today a blessing and a curse — the blessing, if you obey the commands of the Lord your God. . .; the curse, if you disobey the commands of the Lord your God and turn from the way I command you. . ." (Deut 11:26-28). We can see clearly that if we obey God, we will be blessed with spiritual, emotional and even physical and eternal health and happiness. If we disobey Him, we will be cursed with spiritual, emotional and even eternal ruin. We choose for ourselves. Heaven here and hereafter, or hell. If we say yes, we will live in the kingdom of God, even here on earth. If we say no, we will live in the dark and sinful kingdom of this world under the control of evil.

No One Is Perfect
Actually, no one is perfect enough to always say yes to God. Sometimes we obey, and sometimes we disobey. When we obey, we are blessed. When we disobey, we are cursed with a sadness and suffering that such rebellion causes. In short, we choose our own hell.

Redemption
The good news is that despite our many disobediences, we can always repent, be forgiven and be redeemed. And God will draw even good from our rebellion. Our sins can make us humble, more reliant upon God's grace, and more compassionate toward the sins of others. For those who love God, everything works out for the

good. Even with our sins, as St. Augustine tells us. . .'God can write straight with crooked lines,' and often times does.

Stages of Holiness

Purgative

The first stage of holiness is purgative. Most people go from a life of sin to initial conversion. They enter what is called the purgative stage when they begin to allow God to deal with their ego and their sins. They accept Jesus. They let go and let God. And they begin to say yes to Him — yes to prayer, yes to Sunday Mass, yes to love and forgiveness. In this initial stage of holiness, they still fail many, many times. But if they are faithful, they will go deeper and enter into a second phase of holiness.

Illuminative

The second phase is called the illuminative phase. People in this stage begin to go to Mass even on a daily basis. They begin to read the Bible daily and to attend a retreat from time to time. Maybe they join a Bible study group or prayer group. This second phase is called the phase of the more so yes.

Unitive

Once again, if they are faithful, they enter into a deeper phase called the unitive way. Very often they have some mystical experiences. They have traversed from the dark night of the soul and they begin to say mostly yes to God. God has become the very center of their lives. People in this phase have become, in the words of Mother Teresa, the very soul of prayer. God is able to work consistently in and through them with His love, His wisdom and His power. They are fully living life in the Spirit, a life in Christ.

The Divine Will

The deepest phase is to be so transformed by God that you live in His will. People in this most purified of stages have received the "gift of the Divine Will." Blessings flow through them all the time. They have become a yes just as Jesus became a yes. "To all the many promises of God, Jesus is the yes to them all" (2 Cor 1:18-20).

Six Stages of Evil in America

First Stage: Normal Goodness Mixed with Normal Sinfulness

The first stage — sin — is the stage the United States was in from its beginning in 1776 to 1962. We were a nation under God and were the recipient of many, many blessings. Not only were we the most blessed of nations, but we prospered as no nation had ever done before. Nevertheless, during this time, we increasingly sinned and, in many ways, lost the blessing. In fact, from 1900 to 1941, sin in America doubled as we began to condone sinful ways. We did not listen to God's warnings and we saw the rise of communism and a second world war worse than the first. Both of these came as curses because of our sinfulness.

Second Stage: Reject Godliness, Embrace Humanism

Then in 1962 we entered into a second phase when we began to reject God and His laws. We began to rationalize our sin. We allowed five members of our Supreme Court to take away our cherished Biblical foundation and to contradict our Constitution which clearly states, "Congress shall make no law prohibiting the free exercise of religion." Our Supreme Court, with our tacit permission, forbade prayer in public schools and in subsequent rulings the Supreme Court prohibited Bible reading, religious symbols and religious songs, as well.

Secular humanism became the official religion of America as we made man, not God, the measure of all things. But worse than that, we began to rationalize our rejection of God. We instituted a new interpretation of separation of Church and state and made it sound so American. Many Americans followed the philosophy of the American Civil Liberties Union and The People of the American Way. And we made it sound so patriotic.

Third Stage: Denial of Right to Life

A third phase was entered after 1973 when our Supreme Court

stated we could no longer "hold these truths to be self-evident, that all men" (including the unborn) "were endowed by our Creator with certain inalienable rights"; first and foremost, the right to "life", as well as "liberty and the pursuit of happiness". And we began the wholesale destruction of babies in the womb. To date, we have murdered 100 million of them. We justified it by calling it "choice". We justified other sins, as well. No longer would we call it sodomy — we now called it alternative lifestyles. No longer was it immorality and adultery — it was now called consenting adults. No longer was it pornography — it was now called first amendment rights. We turned America upside down — what was bad was now good, and what was good was now bad. And the new enemy of America became the Old Guard, that is orthodox Christians and Jews.

A Fourth Stage - Bragged About Evil

A fourth stage then entered America during which people bragged about their sins. People marched and carried banners promoting sodomy, abortion and immorality. Filth entered our media and infiltrated the Internet. The new heroes were those in the entertainment industry living flagrantly immoral lives, while talk show hosts promoted violence, immorality and vulgarity.

A Fifth Stage - We Attacked God and His Church

Then beginning in the '90s, we attacked the good. We stated that the real problem was Jesus and His Church. They were "intolerant" of our sins. They were the new enemies of the American Way. Our liberal and permissive press took on an aggressive anti-Christian and anti-Catholic bias. Theologically, this phase is called "the sin against the Holy Spirit." It is, in the teachings of Jesus, the only unforgivable sin because, in and through it, we reject not only the Savior of the world, but also His saving plan to form a Mystical Body called the Church.

A Sixth Stage - Chastisement

The sixth stage, of course, is God's judgment, which has already begun. God's prophets all over the world have been warning us for almost two decades that a time of chastisement and judgment would come upon America if we did not repent and turn back to God.

Then September 11th

Then came September 11th and we saw America shaken to its roots. From the president to the mayor of New York, from the governor to the policemen and firefighters on the streets, we saw people at prayer and even churches that were crowded throughout the nation. Millions of Americans were driven to their knees. And from the White House to ground zero, from the Capitol to Yankee Stadium, prayerful people joined hands and sang, "God Bless America." Intuitively, Americans realized that we are a nation under God and we cannot survive without His Providence.

3

A Nation Under God

America's Founding Fathers believed that a widespread faith in God was the true source of America's greatness. They would see today's war against Christianity by our government, our educational institutions, the media and throughout the popular culture as a grave threat to America's survival as a free nation.

Our Founding Fathers

Historically the United States of America is a Christian nation because our Founding Fathers were almost to a man professing Christians. Fifty-two of the fifty-five Founding Fathers who worked on the Constitution were Christians. They founded this nation upon the Judaic-Christian ethic.

Judaic-Christian Ethic

When we say that America was founded according to the Judaic-Christian ethic we mean that biblical tenets were the basis of all of our founding documents, laws, moral codes and institutions. A portion of the charter for the Virginia colony stated: "To the glory of his Divine Majesty, and propagating of the Christian religion to such people as yet live in ignorance of the true knowledge and worship of God."

Mayflower Compact

When the pilgrims signed the Mayflower Compact, they declared: "For the glory of God and advancement of ye Christian faith. . . doe by these presence solemnly and mutually in ye presence of God and one of another, covenant and combine ourselves together into a civil body politick."

De Tocqueville

When Alexis De Tocqueville wrote his famous books on the great experiment in democracy by the United States, he stated, "In the United States of America the sovereign authority is religious... There is no other country in the world in which the Christian religion retains a greater influence over the souls of men than in America."

Lincoln

Abraham Lincoln, perhaps our greatest president next to Washington and the man who kept our nation together, declared: "In regard to this Great Book, I have but to say, it is the best gift God has given to man. All the good the Saviour gave to the world was communicated through this book. But for it, we would not know right from wrong. All things most desirable for man's welfare, here and hereafter, are to be found portrayed in it."

Most Precedented Statement

In 1892, the United States Supreme Court in its most precedented statement (actually giving 87 precedents to the statement in a 16-page decision), boldly declared, *"Our laws and our institutions must necessarily be based upon and embody the teachings of the Redeemer of mankind. It is impossible that it should be otherwise; and in this sense and to this extent our civilization and our institutions are emphatically Christian. . . this is a religious people. This is historically true. From the discovery of this conti-*

nent to the present hour, there is a single voice making this affirmation. . . we find everywhere a clear definition of the same truth. . . this is a Christian nation." (Church of the Holy Trinity vs. United States, 143 US457, 36L ed226, Justice Brewer)

Nature's God

"When in the course of human events it becomes necessary for one people to dissolve the political bands which have connected them to another and to assume among the powers of the earth, the separate and equal station to which the laws of nature and of nature's God entitles them, a decent respect to the opinions of mankind requires that they should declare the causes which impel them to the separation."

Those are the words written by Thomas Jefferson in the Declaration of Independence. And the most important of these words to the Founding Fathers were those that declared the rights endowed to all mankind by "nature's God".

From the foundation of our country, America has relied on God and the rights bequeathed to us by Him. Thomas Jefferson made that crystal clear when he cited "nature's God" in the Declaration of Independence. And the other founding Fathers made it equally clear in the Constitution of the United States when they guaranteed religious freedom in the First Amendment. But what is "nature's God", and what rights are granted by Him? The Founding Fathers clearly believed that nature was created by God, and that the Holy Scriptures contained the laws of God and the rights given to man by God.

From the time this country was founded, it was understood by our leaders that God had granted us certain rights that no government should curtail. It was also understood that, in order to continue to be a good and just nation in the eyes of the Lord, America needed to maintain that Christian heritage and give thanks to God for granting it to us. One of the first official acts of that Congress was to open with a prayer. Virtually every President, upon taking the oath of office, invoked God in one way or another and asked Him to guide our nation. Congress also established a National Day of Thanksgiving, praising God for granting our young nation its freedom.

But today, opponents of faith and prayer outrageously assert that the Founding Fathers actually meant to strike God from the public domain when they approved the First Amendment to the Constitution. Such an assertion is blatantly false. The Founding Fathers explained that the First Amendment was merely to prevent a single denomination from being federally established. The Founders wanted to avoid in America what had occurred in Great Britain, when everyone—by government decree—was forced to become Anglican. Even the most superficial examination makes it clear that the Founding Fathers were devoutly religious men, and wanted their nation to be devoutly religious as well

4
One Nation Under God. What does this mean?

It means that we recognize this land, this flag and this government as a gift from God to be used for His purposes.

It means that we did not become the land of the free and the home of the brave by blind faith or a happy set of circumstances. Rather, that a wise and loving God was hovering over us from the very hour of our conception.

It means that Columbus, under the direct inspiration of the Holy Spirit, discovered this land, placed a cross in his hands, planted it in the soil, fell upon his knees and took possession of this land for God.

It means that faith in God guided the Mayflower as it chartered the treacherous Atlantic.

It means that old George Washington in his farewell address stated, "Whereas it is the duty of all nations to acknowledge the providence of Almighty God, to obey His will, to be grateful for His benefits and humbly implore His protection and favor. . ."

It means that as our Founding Fathers stated, "for the support of this declaration of Independence, with a firm reliance on the protection of Divine Providence, we mutually pledge to each other, our lives, our fortunes, and our sacred honor."

It means that as Noah Webster stated, "The religion which has introduced civil liberty in our nation is a religion of Christ and His apostles. To this we owe our free constitutions of government."

It means that as Patrick Henry stated, "It cannot be emphasized too clearly or too often that this great nation was founded, not by religionists but by Christians, not on religions but on the gospel of Jesus Christ."

It means that our founding fathers had no intention of separating state from God. From a particular church, yes; but from God never. They stated, "By our form of government, the Christian religion is the established religion; and all sects and denominations of Christians are placed on the same equal footing." (Runkel vs. Winemiller, Maryland Supreme Court, 1799)

It means that the New England Primer—the first textbook for our public schools, that served from 1690 and for the next 200 years as the textbook for American schools—was read like a Bible. Some examples:

A. "A wise son makes a glad father."

B. "Better is having little with fear of the Lord than having great treasure."

C. "Come unto Christ all ye that labor and are heavy laden and He will give you rest."

It means that the first 108 colleges in this country were all Christian schools, including Harvard, Yale, Princeton, and William and Mary.

It means that as John Quincy Adams stated: "the birthday of our nation is indissolubly linked with the birthday of our Savior. That is why the Fourth of July is, next to Christmas, our most joyous and most venerated festival."

It means that as John Jay, the original Chief Justice of the Supreme Court, stated: "Providence has given to our people the choice of their rulers, and it is the duty as well as the privilege of our Christian nation to prefer Christians for their rulers."

It means that as Abraham Lincoln stated, "It is the duty of nations, as well as of men, to owe their independence upon the overruling power of God and to recognize this divine truth announced in the holy scriptures and proven in all history, that those nations only are blessed whose God is the Lord."

It means that as Woodrow Wilson stated: "the Bible is the one supreme source of revelation of the meaning of life, the nature of God, and the spiritual nature and need of men, the only God of life which leads the Spirit of peace and salvation."

It means that as John Kennedy stated, "Let us go forward asking God's blessing, but realizing here on earth God's work is truly our own."

It means as George W. Bush quoted, "That neither death, nor life nor angels nor principalities can separate us from the love of God."

It means that "we are met in a great battlefield testing whether this nation or as Abraham Lincoln stated any nation so conceived and so dedicated can long endure." We must confess with humble hearts that before September 11th, 2001, a day that will live in infamy, much of America had forgotten God.

Like Nazi Germany, Communist Russia, and Fascist Italy, we had declared that religion, prayer and God had no place in our government (1962); and that human life was no longer sacred (1973). This in the land that still believes these truths to be self evident that all men are endowed by their Creator with certain inalienable rights, first and foremost the right to life—from the moment of conception to the moment of natural death.

Abortion — The Killing of the Innocent

Communism was guilty of murdering 100 million people, but so have we — through abortion. Twelve million Jewish people have been killed, twice as many as Nazi Germany. Twenty million black people, double those killed in the slave trade have been lost through abortion. And 50 million women have been denied life in a country that boasts of women's rights. How can anybody be a feminist if they do not grant a woman's right to exist. For 'to be, or not to be,' that is always the ultimate question.

9/11/01

Before 9/11 — a day that will divide our modern history — America was rolling in luxuries, reveling in excesses, rollicking in pleasure, revolting in morals, and rotting in sin. We had become a society in which passions had become riderless horses, in which pornography and prostitution went unchecked; in which there was a desolation of decency, wherein love had become a jungled emotion and lust was exalted to lordship.

A Drastic Change

Now, all that has changed. America is once again at prayer and Americans are singing, "God Bless America." God, once again, has our attention. He still warns us that it is sheer folly to suppose that the strength and security of our country lies in our military might, our diplomatic skills, our industrial prowess, or our scientific ingenuity. Our real defense as a nation is in Him and in the convictions, character and commitments of those who are willing to follow Him.

Our Forefathers

Our forefathers warned that our Constitution was good only so long as the Lord is our God. The second verse of our national anthem, so proudly sung, still reads, "Blessed with victory and peace may this heaven-rescued land praise the Power that hath made and preserved us a nation. Then conquer we must, when our cause it is just, and this be our motto, 'In God Be Our Trust.' And the Star Spangled Banner, in triumph shall wave, o'er the land of the free and the home of the brave."

God's Promise

God is promising us, "If my people, who were called by my name will humble themselves and pray and seek my presence and turn away from their evil ways, I will hear from heaven and will forgive their sins and heal their land." (2 Chron 7:14). And, "I will make their enemies to be at peace with them."

Faith of Our Fathers

We are returning to the faith of our fathers and becoming, once again, a nation under God. Something marvelous and wonderful is happening in the soul of our nation. The choice is clearer than ever. It is repent or perish, revival or ruin, God's vision, or ours.

The Real Terrorists

The real terrorists are not simply those of the Middle East, but those who have, for three generations, been destroying the twin pillars of our country — religion and morality — as identified by Washington. The question of the hour is: Will we be, once again, a nation under God with our enemies at peace with us, or still under attack? From without, yes, but more fearfully, from within. Under God or under attack? The choice is clear.

5

What Does Our Flag Stand For
- The Foundations of American Government

Day of Infamy

Since September 11, 2001—a day of infamy—Americans have been reeling in aftershock. The cause? Terrorism. The sight of terrorism in our own country. The reaction has been a nation at prayer, a nation united, a nation supportive of its president, and a nation with new respect for its flag. For what it has done is to shake America to its roots.

Our Roots

What are our roots? What is it that makes us the land of the free and the home of the brave? What does it mean that we are a nation 'under God'? What does it means "that we hold these truths to be self-evident that all men are endowed by our Creator with certain inalienable rights"—first of all, to life, and then to liberty and the pursuit of happiness.

Laws of Nature and Laws of Nature's God

Let us together look at our roots. We say that we are a nation under God because our 243 Founding Fathers established us that way. 94 percent of all existing quotations of our Founding Fathers came from the Bible. Our government was based upon "the laws of nature and the laws of nature's God," words that we find in the Bill of Rights.

Blackstone's Law Commentary

Blackstone's commentary on law, which was the official commentary on American law from the time of our forefathers all the way into the middle of the 20th century, read like the Bible. In our first colleges, which were all Christian, each student was required to read the Bible, attend chapel service, and live by the standards of Christian morality.

New England Primer

The New England Primer, which read like a Catechism, was the official textbook in all schools, from that time to the 20th century. In fact, in the 19th century, people were arrested for blaspheming the name of Jesus. And both the lower court and the Supreme Court called it treason.

A Curriculum Without Christ?

Also in the 19th century, a certain school wanted to have a curriculum without religious content. Both the House of Representatives and the Senate rejected it, questioning, 'How could you teach students wisdom without God as the source of wisdom? How could you teach them to be holy without the Spirit of God that we call holy?'

Our Religious Heritage

Our heritage is undeniably religious. Beginning with the first primarily Catholic explorers—Marquette, Vasco de Gama, Isaac Joques, Junipero Serra, Ponce de Leon, Christopher Columbus—and moving on to the pilgrims, the American Revolution, the Civil War and long after, religion had the strongest positive influence on the successful development of this nation.

Compton's Encyclopedia

Compton's Encyclopedia states, "The most powerful, single influence in all history has been Christianity. This influence has shown itself not only in religious beliefs and spiritual ideals of the human race, but in the march of political events and institutions, as well" (vol. 3, pg. 301).

We are surrounded with recognitions of our Judaic-Christian roots. Even our money declares our faith in God, for it is imprinted with our national motto, "In God We Trust." Our Pledge of Allegiance heralds our testimony to God's importance: "And to the Republic for which it stands, one nation under God, indivisible, with liberty and justice for all."

Supreme Court

In 1892, the Supreme Court stated, "The laws and institutions of this nation must necessarily be based upon and embodied in the life and teachings of the Redeemer of mankind. It is impossible that it should be otherwise."

In 1931, Supreme Court Justice George Sutherland reviewed the 1892 decision in another case and reiterated that Americans are a "Christian people". And in 1952, Justice William O. Douglas, affirmed that, "We are a religious people and our institutions presuppose a Supreme Being."

Public Education

One of the arenas in which the Judaic-Christian ethic was most visible was in American public education. Our nation's first schools were in churches, and for more than three centuries, following their inception in the mid-1600s, public schools promoted prayer and regularly used the Bible as a textbook. Traditional Judaic-Christian principles were the firm basis for teaching morals. Students trained in these public schools were well rounded and well equipped in mind, soul, spirit and body. Noah Webster, a Founding Father and leading educator, accurately reflected this when he stated,

"No truth is more evident to my mind than that the Christian religion must be the basis of any government intended to secure the rights and privileges of a few people."

Benjamin Rush

Benjamin Rush, a signer of the Declaration of Independence and the first Founder to call for free public schools, similarly explained:

[T]he only foundation for a useful education in a republic is to be laid in religion. Without this there can be no virtue, and without virtue there can be no liberty, and liberty is the object and life of all republican governments. . . Without religion, I believe learning does much mischief to the morals and principles of mankind."

Benjamin Franklin

From its inception, our nation had believed in the power and the results of religious teachings and practices and had strongly supported their inclusion in public arenas. Revered national political leaders believed that public prayer could and would change the course of the nation. For example, consider Benjamin Franklin's lengthy speech delivered at the Constitutional Convention. The nation's elder statesman and patriarch (and today considered to be one of the least religious of the Founding Fathers) reminded the other delegates:

"In the beginning of the contest with Britain, when we were sensible of danger, we had daily prayers in this room for Divine protection. Our prayers, Sir, were heard, and they were graciously answered. All of us who were engaged in the struggle must have observed frequent instances of a superintending Providence in our favor. . . And have we now forgotten this powerful Friend? Or do we imagine we no longer need His assistance? I have lived, Sir, a long time, and the longer I live, the more convincing proofs I see of this truth: 'that God governs in the affairs of man.' And if the sparrow cannot fall to the ground without His notice, is it probable that an empire can rise without His aid? For we have been assured, Sir, in the Sacred Writings that except the Lord build the house, they labor in vain that build it. I firmly believe this. I also believe that without His concurring aid, we shall succeed in the political building no better than the builders of Babel; we shall be divided by our little, partial local interests; our projects will be confounded; and we ourselves shall become a reproach and a byword down to future ages. And what is worse, mankind may hereafter from this unfortunate instance, despair of establishing government by human wisdom and leave it to chance, war, or conquest. I therefore beg leave to move that, henceforth, prayers imploring the assistance of Heaven and its blessing on our deliberation be held in this assembly every morning before we proceed to business."

God Blessed Us

As Franklin noted, God had often answered their prayers and manifested Himself throughout the struggle with Great Britain; He blessed their efforts at the Constitutional Convention no less—a fact noted by many of the Founders, including Benjamin Rush:

"I do not believe that the Constitution was the offspring of inspiration, but I am as perfectly satisfied that the Union of the States in its form and adoption is as much the work of a Divine Providence as any of the miracles recorded in the Old and New Testament."

New Godly State Constitution

Consequently, they returned home from Philadelphia to their own states and began to create new state constitutions. Samuel Adams and John Adams helped write the Massachusetts constitution; Benjamin Rush and James Wilson helped write Pennsylvania's constitution; George Read and Thomas McKean helped write Delaware's constitution; the same was true in other states as well. It is significant to note that the Supreme Court formerly pointed to these state constitutions as precedents to demonstrate the Founders' intent.

Delaware

Notice, for example, what Thomas McKean and George Read placed in the Delaware constitution:

Every person, who shall be chosen a member of either house, or appointed to any office or place of trust. . . shall. . . make and subscribe the following declaration, to wit: "I do profess faith in God the father, and in Jesus Christ, his only son, and in the Holy Ghost, one God, blessed forever more, and I do acknowledge the Holy Scriptures of the Old and New Testament to be given by divine inspiration."

While today we wish this were the requirement for seminary, it was their requirement for politics! Yet, take note of their emphasis: the focus is on the type of individuals placed into office, not on the type of laws.

Notice Some Other State Constitutions:

Pennsylvania

The Pennsylvania constitution authored by Benjamin Rush and James Wilson declared:

"And each member [of this legislature], before he takes his seat, shall make and subscribe the following declaration, viz: "I do believe in one God, the Creator and Governor of the universe, the rewarder of the good and the punisher of the wicked, and I do acknowledge the Scriptures of the Old and New Testament to be given by Divine Inspiration.""

Massachusetts

The Massachusetts constitution, authored by Samuel Adams (the Father of the American Revolution) and John Adams, stated:

[All persons elected must] make and subscribe the following declaration, viz. "I do declare that I believe the Christian religion and have firm persuasion of its truth."

North Carolina

North Carolina's constitution required that:

"No person, who shall deny the being of God, or the truth of the [Christian] religion, or the divine authority either of the Old or New Testaments, or who shall hold religious principles incompatible with the freedom and safety of the State, shall be capable of holding any office, or place of trust or profit in the civil department, within this State."

What a powerful declaration! You had to believe that God's principles applied to civil government or they wouldn't let you near public office!

Connecticut

This belief in the importance of God-fearing leaders was so well understood in America that in 1892, the Supreme Court pointed out that of the forty-four States that were then in the Union, each had some type of God-centered declaration in its constitution.

From Government to Education

Our Founding Fathers went to great lengths to ensure that we never forgot the principles of sound government. As many of them grew older, they realized that when they died, America would also die with them—unless they were able to transmit to subsequent generations the principles upon which they had built America's government. For this reason, many Founding Fathers became intimately involved with education. In fact, so important was education to the Founding Fathers that in the ten years following the American Revolution, more colleges were established in America than in the 150 years preceding the Revolution!

Noah Webster

Noah Webster was one of the many Founding Fathers who became an educator. Webster served not only as a soldier during the American Revolution but also as a legislator in two states after the Revolution. Additionally, he was one of the first Founding Fathers to call for a Constitutional Convention, and he was personally responsible for Article 1, Section 8, of the Constitution. As an educator, Noah Webster helped establish Amherst College and became one of the most prolific textbook writers of any of the Founding Fathers.

History of the United States

One of his texts, used in American public school classrooms for generations, was his *History of the United States*. In it, he told students:

"When you become entitled to exercise the right of voting for public officers, let it be impressed on your mind that God commands you to choose for rulers, 'just men who will rule in the fear of God.' The preservation of [our] government depends on the faithful discharge of this duty; if the citizens neglect their duty and place unprincipled men in office, the government will soon be corrupted; laws will be made, not for the public good so much as for selfish or local purposes; corrupt or incompetent men will be appointed to execute the laws; the public revenues will be squandered on unworthy men; and the rights of the citizens will be violated or disregarded."

While his description of the ills of government sounds like an excerpt from yesterday's newspaper, this was not occurring in their day but was simply a warning of what would happen if ungodly men were placed into office. Webster then concluded:

"If [our] government fails to secure public prosperity and happiness, it must be because the citizens neglect the divine commands, and elect bad men to make and administer the laws."

Although Noah Webster taught students that our form of government could not survive unless we kept Godly, God-fearing people of faith in office, doesn't the security of our particular form of government really depend upon the people rather than upon their representatives? After all, some might ask, in a democracy, aren't the people the most important element?

A Republic Under God

This is part of our problem today: some think we are a democracy; we are not. When we pledge allegiance to the flag, we pledge allegiance to *the republic* of the United States, not the democracy of the United States. While few today can define the difference between the two, there is a difference—a major difference. In a democracy, whatever the majority of the people desire becomes public policy. If the majority of the people decide that murder, abortion, pornography, adultery, and divorce are allowable, such ills would become public policy. Not so in a republic under God. The aforementioned ills are always against "the laws of nature and the laws of nature's God."

George Washington

George Washington was another of the many Founding Fathers who avidly believed in the importance of prayer. Numerous paintings show "The Father of Our Country" in prayer, including the stained glass window in the U.S. Congressional Chapel and the monument at Valley Forge. Even his first speech after his election as President was marked by his call for prayer:

"It would be peculiarly improper to omit, in this first official act, my fervent supplication to that Almighty Being who rules over the universe, who presides in the councils of nations, and whose providential aids can supply every human defect. . . No people can be bound to acknowledge and adore the invisible hand which conducts the affairs of men more than the people of the United States." He then warned:

"[T]he propitious [favorable] smiles of Heaven can never be expected on a nation that disregards the eternal rules of order and right which Heaven itself has ordained."

Religion and Morality: The Twin Pillars of Our Nation

For eight years, Washington wisely and skillfully guided this nation to a position from which its continued strength and development would be assured. In his "Farewell Address," he warned:

"Of all the dispositions and habits which lead to political prosperity, religion and morality are indispensable supports. In vain would that man claim the tribute of patriotism who should labour to subvert these great pillars of human happiness. . . The mere political, equally with the pious man, ought to respect and to cherish them."

We Cannot Forget God

Franklin had warned that "forgetting God" and imagining that we no longer needed His "concurring aid" would result in internal disputes, the decay of the nation's prestige and reputation, and a diminished national success. Washington had warned that if religious principles were excluded, the nation's morality and political prosperity would suffer. Yet, despite such clear words, in cases beginning in 1962, the Supreme Court offered rulings which effectually divorced the nation, its schools, and its public affairs from more than three centuries of its heritage; America is now learning experientially what both Washington and Franklin knew to be true — we are suffering in the very areas they predicted.

1962 — A New Direction

In decisions rendered on June 25, 1962, in Engle *v.* Vitale, and on June 17, 1963, in Murray *v.* Curlett and Abington *v.* Schempp, the Supreme Court forbade the inclusion of religious practices in major activities of daily student life by striking down school prayer and Bible reading. Never before in the history of our nation had any branch of our government taken such a stand.

Millions Affected

Through those decisions, 39 million students and over 2 million teachers were barred from participating in what had been available to students since our nation's founding. Even today, millions of Americans personally recall when prayer, Bible reading, and religious principles were as much a part of their public school activities as was the study of math or the pursuit of athletics. Activities once considered an integral part of education are now totally censured.

Separation of God from State?

This sudden and dramatic restructuring of educational policies was precipitated by the Court's re-interpretation of the phrase "separation of church and state." The First Amendment does not contain that phrase; it simply states, "Congress shall make no law respecting an establishment of religion, or prohibiting the free exercise thereof." This had always meant that Congress was prohibited from establishing a national religious denomination—e.g., Congress could not pass a law requiring Americans to become Catholics, Anglicans, or members of any specific denomination.

A Different and New Interpretation

This meaning for "separation of church and state" had been explained clearly during the time of the Founders and was applied by the Courts for 170 years afterwards. But, in 1962, the Supreme Court decided that "church" would no longer mean a "federal denomination"; instead, it would now mean a "religious activity in public." Consequently, "separation of church and state" was no longer a prohibition against establishing a national denomination; it was now a prohibition against including religious activities in public affairs.

Contradicts Our Constitution

This new interpretation of "church" immediately invited hundreds of lawsuits challenging any presence of religion in public life. While skyrocketing numbers of lawsuits are still awaiting disposition, courts have already delivered far-reaching decisions to:

Remove student prayer: "Prayer in its public school system breaches the constitution wall of separation between Church and State." Engel *v.* Vitale, 1962

Remove school Bible readings: "[N]o state law or school board may require that passages from the bible be read or that the Lord's Prayer be recited in the public schools of a State at the beginning of each school day." Abington *v.* Schempp, 1963

Remove the Ten Commandments from view: "If the posted copies of the Ten Commandments are to have any effect at all, it will be to induce the schoolchildren to read, meditate upon, perhaps to venerate and obey, the Commandments. . . this. . . is not a permissible state objective under the Establishment Clause." Stone *v.* Graham, 1980.

Remove benedictions and invocations from school activities: "Religious invocation. . . in high school commencement exercise conveyed message that district had given its endorsement to prayer and religion, so that school district was properly [prohibited] from including invocation in commencement exercise." Graham *v.* Central, 1985; Kay *v.* Douglas, 1986; Jager *v.* Douglas, 1989; Lee *v.* Weisman, 1992.

Lower Court Rulings

Lower court rulings have gone even further than those of the Supreme Court, chipping away at the original intent until a religion-hostile attitude is now the norm in many courts. Today, there is such an anti-religious prejudice in education that some courts have forbidden the following activities within their jurisdiction:

Freedom of speech and press is guaranteed to students unless the topic is religious, at which time such speech becomes unconstitutional. Stein *v.* Oshinsky, 1965; Collins *v.* Chandler Unified School District, 1981.

If a student prays over his lunch, it is unconstitutional for him to pray aloud. Reed *v.* Van Hoven, 1965.

It is unconstitutional for a Board of Education to use or refer to the word "God" in any of its official writings. Ohio *v.* Whisner, 1976.

Many state and local officials have gone even further than these courts. For example:

Public schools were barred from showing a film about the settlement of Jamestown because the film depicted the erection of a cross at the settlement, despite the historical fact that a cross was erected at the Jamestown settlement.

In the Alaska public schools, students were told they could not use the word "Christmas" in school because it had the word "Christ" in it, nor could they have the word in their notebooks, nor exchange Christmas cards or presents, nor display anything with the word "Christmas" on it.

In Colorado, a music teacher was stopped from singing traditional Christmas carols in her classes.

From Classroom to Government

These rulings are not without consequence. What occurs in the classroom eventually affects the rest of the nation. As explained by President Abraham Lincoln:

"The philosophy of the classroom in one generation will be the philosophy of government in the next."

The current anti-religious bias in education is new, having been implemented only after the re-definition of the First Amendment in 1962. Only eight years later, the Court acknowledged that it had begun a legal revolution, even admitting that:

"It was . . . not until 1962 that . . . prayers were held to violate the [First Amendment].

The Court further conceded that the decision to remove prayer had been made without any previous precedent, either legal or historical. However, the Court argued that it needed no precedent:

Finally, in Engle *v.* Vitale, only last year, these principles [the separation of prayer from the classroom] were so universally recognized that the Court, without the citation of a single case . . .

reaffirmed them.

The Court attempted to invoke peer pressure to justify its lack of precedent: i.e., "everyone" understands the removal of prayer was necessary. However, the so-called "universally recognized" principles calling for the separation of religious principles from public education were so foreign that many commented on the new and dramatic change.

For example, the 1963 World Book Encyclopedia Yearbook stated: "The significance of the decision regarding this [school] prayer was enormous, for the whole thorny problem of religion in public education was thus inevitably raised."

Notice that prior to this case, the legal issue of separating prayer and religious principles from education had not been "raised." Legal observers also commented on the Court's departure from precedent:

The Court has broken new ground in a number of fields . . . Few Supreme Court decisions of recent years have created greater furor than Engle v. Vitale.

Few professions agreed with the Court that its decisions were based on "universally recognized" principles. In fact, in Zorach v. Clauson, only ten short years before, the Court was still embracing the philosophy it had maintained for over a century-and-a-half, declaring:

"The First Amendment, however, does not say that in every and all respects there shall be a separation of Church and State. . . Otherwise the state and religion would be aliens to each other — hostile, suspicious, and even unfriendly."

How could the 1962 Supreme Court Justices so quickly repudiate nearly two centuries of Supreme Court rulings? How could they have ignored the Court's lengthy history of protecting Christian principles and religious activities in public education? Perhaps the answer rests in the fact that eight of the nine Justices on the 1962-63 Supreme Court had been appointed to the Court following an extended history of political rather than judicial experience.

For example, Chief Justice Earl Warren had been the Governor of California for ten years prior to his appointment; Justice Hugo

Black had been a U.S. Senator for ten years; Justice Felix Frank-furter had been an assistant to the Secretary of Labor and a found-ing member of the ACLU; Justice Arthur Goldberg had been the Secretary of Labor; Justice William Douglas was chairman of the Securities and Exchange Commission prior to his appointment. All of the Justices except one had similar political backgrounds.

Justice Potter Stewart, a federal judge for four years prior to his appointment, was the only member of the court with extended federal constitutional experience prior to his appointment. Inter-estingly, he was also the only justice who objected to the removal of prayer and Bible reading. He alone acted as a judge; the rest acted as politicians, determined to develop new policies rather than to uphold previous precedents.

Those activist justices not only initiated the Christian-hostile policy, they firmly guided and strengthened it during their tenure. However, their anti-religious rulings were by no means limited solely to education. They also caused the reversal of long-standing social policies for children, families, and the nation. In fact, each of these arenas had preserved an extended legal history during which the Court had not only refused to exclude religious principles, but had relied upon them when rendering its decision. The following statements are representative of those which appeared in scores of cases.

"Christianity has referenced to the principles of right and wrong . . . it is the foundation of those morals and manners upon which our society is formed; it is their basis. Remove this and they would fall . . . [Morality] has grown upon the basis of Christianity. . . The day of moral virtue in which we live would, in an instant, if that standard were abolished, lapse into the dark and murky night of pagan immorality." Charleston *v.* Benjamin.

"The morality of the country is deeply engrafted upon Chris-tianity. . . [We are] people whose manners and whose morals have been elevated and inspired by means of the Christian religion." People *v.* Ruggles

The Constitution
Our Constitution was written under the direct blessing of Al-

mighty God, after Benjamin Franklin called for three days of fasting and prayer. Like God, Himself, our Constitution does not force religion but promotes it and in no way oppresses it. Our Founding Fathers did not want one denomination to rule over another. Therefore, they were for the separation of church and state, but never of state from God. In fact, in 1779, the Court declared, "By our form of government, the Christian religion is the established religion; and all sects and denominations of Christians are placed on the same equal footing" (Runkle v. Winemiller, Supreme Court, Maryland, 1799).

George Washington's Warning

In his farewell address, once again, our first president warned that religion and morality were the twin pillars of our country. And anyone who would attack these could not be considered a loyal American. For they are our roots. We, unlike most nations, are a "nation under God". Our motto will always be, "In God We Trust."

Motto Available For Classrooms

Recently, our national motto had been reprinted against the American flag. Since the 11th of September, it has already been placed again in tens of thousands of public school classrooms. Here at My Father's House, we are promoting that. You can get copies of these beautiful large posters by calling (662) 844-5036. They are $100 for 100. This is completely constitutional. It is our national motto.

6
Actual Quotations from
Our Founding Fathers and Our Presidents

I. Our Founding Fathers

George Washington: "It is impossible to rightly govern without God and the Bible."

John Adams: "The general principles upon which our founders achieved independence. . .were the principles of Christianity."

Andrew Jackson: "The Bible is the rock upon which our republic rests."

James Madison: "Religion is the basis and foundation of government."

John Adams: "Religion and virtue are the only foundations of free government."

Patrick Henry: "It cannot be emphasized too strongly or too often that this great nation was founded. . .by Christians; not on religions, but on the Gospel of Jesus Christ. The Bible is worth all other books that have ever been printed."

Abraham Lincoln: "The Bible is the best gift God ever gave to man."

John Quincy Adams: "From the day of the Declaration. . .(the American people) were bound by the laws of God, which they all acknowledge as the rules of their conduct."

James Madison: "A nation that will not be ruled by the Ten Commandments, shall be ruled by tyrants."

James Monroe: "The liberty, prosperity and happiness of our country will always be the object of my most fervent prayers to the Supreme Author of All Good."

William Penn: "Let men be good and government cannot be bad."

James Madison: "The future of America rests not in the laws of this Constitution, but in the laws of God."

II. God and the Presidents

Clearly our Founding Fathers were deeply religious men, who took their faith seriously and who used Christian principles to build a nation. But it wasn't just our Founding Fathers who demonstrated their strong Christian faith. From George Washington to George W. Bush, our U.S. Presidents have nearly unanimously invoked God when embarking upon their presidencies.

George Washington, 1789

". . .the benign Parent of the Human Race. . .has been pleased to favor the American people with opportunities" for "the security of their union and the advancement of their happiness. . ." "The success of this Government must depend" upon "His divine blessing".

John Adams, 1797

Invoking the Supreme Being, "Patron of Order, Fountain of Justice, and Protector in all ages. . .of virtuous liberty" to continue "His blessing upon this nation. . .and give it all possible success and duration consistent with the ends of His providence."

Thomas Jefferson, 1801

"May that Infinite Power which rules the destinies of the universe lead our councils to do what is best. . .for peace and prosperity."

Jefferson, 1805

Beseeched "that Being in whose hands we are. . .who has covered our infancy with His providence and our riper years with His wisdom and power" . . .so that "He will so enlighten. . .your servants, guide their councils" so they shall do "your good" and secure "the peace, friendship, and approbation of all nations."

James Madison, 1809

Beseeched "the guidance of that Almighty Being whose power regulates the destiny of nations, whose blessings" have enriched "this rising Republic."

James Monroe, 1817
Invoked "the Almighty that He will. . .continue. . .that protection. . . He has already so conspicuously displayed."

Monroe, 1821
". . .firm reliance on the protection of Almighty God. . ."

John Quincy Adams, 1825
Invoked the Lord's favor and "His overruling providence."

Andrew Jackson, 1829
Expressed reliance on "the Power whose providence mercifully protected our nation's infancy, and has since upheld our liberties" and beseeched Him to "continue to make our beloved country the object of His divine care."

Jackson, 1833
Beseeched "that Almighty Being" to "overrule all my intentions and actions and inspire the hearts of my fellow citizens that we may be preserved from dangers. . .and continue forever as a united and happy people."

Martin Van Buren, 1837
Beseeched "His providence to bless our beloved country with honors and with length of days."

William Henry Harrison, 1841
Expressed "profound reverence to the Christian religion," convinced that "sound morals, religious liberty, and a just sense of religious respectability are essentially connected with all true and lasting happiness" and commends us to "that good Being who has blessed us by the gifts of civil and religious liberty."

James K. Polk, 1845
Invoked "that Divine Being" who has protected us and beseeched his continued "benedictions."

Zachary Taylor, 1849
Invoked "the goodness (and protection) of Divine Providence."

Franklin Pierce, 1853
Invoked "the kind Providence" which enabled us to preserve our blessings.

James Buchanan, 1857
Invoked "the blessings of Divine Providence."

Abraham Lincoln, 1861
Speaking of opponents dissatisfied with the government, Lincoln called for "Intelligence, patriotism, Christianity, and a firm reliance on Him who has never yet forsaken this favored land. . ."

Lincoln, 1865
Both sides in the conflict "read the same Bible and pray to the same God, and each invokes His aid against the other. It may seem strange that any men should dare to ask a just God's assistance in wringing their bread from the sweat of other men's faces, but let us judge not, that we be not judged. The prayers of both could not be answered. That of neither has been answered fully. The Almighty has His own purposes. 'Woe unto the world because of offenses [and] woe to that man by whom the offense cometh.' If we shall suppose that American slavery is one of those offenses which, in the providence of God, must needs come, but which having continued through His appointed time, He now wills to remove, and that He gives to both North and South this terrible war as the woe due to those [who commit the offense], shall we discern therein any departure from those divine attributes which believers in a living God always ascribe to Him? Fondly do we hope, fervently do we pray, that this mighty scourge of war may speedily pass away."

"With malice toward none, with charity for all, with firmness in the right as God gives us to see the right, let us strive to finish the work we are in, to bind up the nation's wounds, to care for him who shall have borne the battle and for his widow and his orphan, to do all which may achieve and cherish a just and lasting peace among ourselves and with all nations."

Ulysses S. Grant, 1869
Invoked "Almighty God" to heal the nation.

Rutherford B. Hayes, 1877
Invoked "guidance of that Divine Hand by which the destinies of all nations and individuals are shaped" so that "'peace and happiness, truth and justice, religion and piety, may be established among us for all generations.'"

James A. Garfield, 1881
"I reverently invoke the support and blessings of Almighty God" for the "welfare of this great people."

Grover Cleveland, 1885
Invoked aid and blessings of "Almighty God, who presides over the destiny of nations. . ."

Benjamin Harrison, 1889
"God has placed upon our head a diadem and laid at our feet power and wealth beyond definition or calculation," a beacon of hope for the freedom of all peoples.

Cleveland, 1893
"A Supreme Being who rules the affairs of men and nations. . . will not turn from us now if we humbly and reverently seek His powerful aid."

William McKinley, 1897
Swore "before the Lord Most High;" to seek by "constant prayer" to discharge "my solemn responsibilities".

Theodore Roosevelt, 1902
In celebration of Thanksgiving Day 1902, President Theodore Roosevelt wrote, "Rarely has any people enjoyed greater prosperity than we are now enjoying. For this we render heartfelt and solemn thanks to the Giver of Good; and we seek to praise Him—not by words only—but by deeds, by the way in which we do our duty to ourselves and to our fellow men."

William H. Taft, 1909

Sought the "aid of Almighty God in the discharge of my responsible duties."

Woodrow Wilson, 1913

"I summon all honest men, all patriotic, all forward-looking men, to my side. God helping me, I will not fail them. . ."

Wilson, 1917

Invoked "God's Providence" to purge fractional divisions of party and private interests and "I pray God I may be given the wisdom and prudence to do my duty."

Warren G. Harding, 1921

Spoke of "the God-given destiny of our Republic," was "answerable to God and country," and implored the "favor and guidance of God in His Heaven." I have taken the oath on "that passage of Holy Writ: 'What doeth the Lord require of thee but to do justly, and to love mercy, and to walk humbly with thy God?' This I plight to God and country."

Calvin Coolidge, 1925

"America seeks no earthly empire built on blood and force. . . The legions which we send forth are armed, not with the sword, but with the cross. . .all mankind [is] of divine origin. She cherishes no purpose save to merit the favor of Almighty God."

Herbert Hoover, 1929

"I ask the help of Almighty God."

Franklin D. Roosevelt, 1933

Asked "the blessing of God. . .May He guide me in the days to come."

Roosevelt, 1937

Asked "Divine guidance to help us each and every one. . ."

Roosevelt, 1941
"As Americans, we go forward, in the service of our country, by the will of God."

Roosevelt, 1945
"The Almighty God has blessed our land [and has given us] a faith which has become the hope of all peoples in an anguished world. So we pray to Him [for] the achievement of His will."

Harry S. Truman, 1949
"Steadfast in our faith in the Almighty, we will advance toward a world where man's freedom is secure. . . With God's help, the future of mankind will be assured in a world of justice, harmony, and peace."

Dwight D. Eisenhower, 1953
In this "century of trial" we pray to "Almighty God."

John F. Kennedy, 1961
"Asking His blessing and His help. . .knowing that here on earth God's work must truly be our own."

Lyndon B. Johnson, 1965
"But we have no promise from God that our greatness will endure. Democracy rests on faith [and] the judgment of God is harshest on those who are most favored."

Richard M. Nixon, 1969
"As the Apollo astronauts flew over the moon's gray surface on Christmas Eve. . .we heard them invoke God's blessing on [the earth's] goodness. . .let us go forward, firm in our faith [and] sustained by our confidence in the will of God and the promise of man."

Nixon, 1973
"Sustained by our faith in God who created us, and striving always to serve His purposes."

Gerald Ford (not elected, no inauguration)

Jimmy Carter, 1977
No reference, but took oath of office on Bible opened to passage "What does the Lord require of thee, but to do justly, and to love mercy, and to walk humbly with thy God."

Ronald Reagan, 1981
"With God's help, we can and will resolve" our problems. "God bless you."

Reagan, 1985
We stand today "One people under God. . ." We have moved "toward the 'brotherhood of man' that God intended for us." ". . . may He continue to hold us close. . .one people under God, dedicated" to freedom. "God bless you and may God bless America."

George Bush, 1989
"My first act as President is a prayer. I ask you to bow your heads: Heavenly Father, accept our thanks for the peace that yields this day. . .Make us strong to do Your work, willing to heed and hear Your will. . .We are given power not to advance our own purposes. . .There is but one just use of power, and it is to serve people. Help us to remember it, Lord. Amen." "God bless you and God bless the United States of America."

Bill Clinton, 1993
"The Scripture says, 'And let us not be weary in well-doing.'" "With God's help, we must answer the call. . .God bless you all."

Clinton, 1997
"May God strengthen our hands for the good work ahead, and always, always bless our America."

George W. Bush, 2001
"I know this is in our reach because we are guided by a power larger than ourselves who creates us equal in His image."

SOURCE: Wake Up America! The Ongoing War on Christian America, by Kip Caudill

7
Prayers and Proclamations
of United States Presidents

"Almighty God: We make our earnest prayer that Thou wilt keep the United States in Thy holy protection: that Thou wilt incline the hearts of the citizens to cultivate a spirit of subordination and obedience to government, and entertain a brotherly affection and love for one another and for their fellow citizens of the United States at large.

And finally, that Thou wilt most graciously be pleased to dispose us all to do justice, to love mercy, and to demean ourselves with that charity, humility and pacific temper of mind which were the characteristics of the Divine Author of our blessed religion, and without a humble imitation of whose example in these things we can never hope to be a happy nation."

Grant our supplication, we beseech Thee, through Jesus Christ our Lord. Amen.
—**George Washington**

"Hold fast to the Bible as the sheet anchor of your liberties; white its precepts on your heart and practice them in your lives. To the influence of this Book we are indebted for the progress made, and to this we must look as our guide in the future."
—**Ulysses S. Grant**

"I pray God I may be given the wisdom and the prudence to do my duty in the true spirit of this great people."
—**Woodrow Wilson**

"In entering upon this great office I must humbly invoke the God of our fathers for wisdom and firmness to execute its high and responsible duties in such a manner as to restore harmony and ancient friendship among the people of the several States and to pre-

serve our free institutions throughout many generations."
—**James Buchanan**

"So we pray to Him now for the vision to see our way clearly—
to see the way that leads to a better life for ourselves and for all our
fellow men—to the achievement of His will to peace on earth."
—**Franklin D. Roosevelt**

"Almighty God, as we stand here, at this moment, my future
associates in the executive branch of the government join me in
beseeching that Thou will make full and complete our dedication
to the service of the people in this throng and their fellow citizens
everywhere.

"Give us, we pray, the power to discern clearly right from wrong
and allow all our works and actions to be governed thereby and by
the laws of this land."

"Especially we pray that our concern shall be for all the people,
regardless of station, race, or calling. May cooperation be permitted and be the mutual aim of those who, under the concept of our
Constitution, hold to differing political beliefs, so that all may work
for the good of our beloved country and for Thy glory. Amen."
—**Dwight Eisenhower**

"I would like to have my frequent prayer answered that God
let my life be meaningful in the enhancement of His kingdom and
that my life might be meaningful in the enhancement of the lives
of my fellow human beings."
—**Jimmy Carter**

"Today, we utter no prayer more fervently than the ancient
prayer for peace on Earth."
—**Ronald Reagan**

"Heavenly Father, we bow our heads and thank You for Your
love. Accept our thanks for the peace that yields this day and the
shared faith that makes its continuance likely. Make us strong to
do Your work, willing to heed and hear Your will, and write on our

hearts these words: 'Use power to help people.' For we are given power not to advance our own purposes, nor to make a great show in the world, nor a name. There is but one just use of power, and it is to serve people. Help us to remember it, Lord. Amen."
—George Bush

National day of Prayer Proclamation
By the President of the United States of America
A Proclamation April 26, 2002

Since our Nation's founding, Americans have turned to prayer for inspiration, strength, and guidance. In times of trial, we ask God for wisdom, courage, direction, and comfort. We offer thanks for the countless blessing God has provided. And we thank God for sanctifying every human life by creating each of us in His image. As we observe this National Day of Prayer, we call upon the Almighty to continue to bless America and her people.

Especially since September 11, millions of Americans have been led to prayer. They have prayed for comfort in a time of grief, for understanding in a time of danger, and for protection in a time of uncertainty. We have all seen God's great faithfulness to our county. America's enemies sought to weaken and destroy us through acts of terror. None of us would ever wish on anyone what happened on September 11th. Yet tragedy and sorrow none of us would choose have brought forth wisdom, courage, and generosity. In the face of terrorist attacks, prayer provided Americans with hope and strength for the journey ahead.

God has blessed our Nation beyond measure. We give thanks for our families and loved ones, for the abundance of our land and the fruits of labor, for our inalienable rights and liberties, and for a great Nation that leads the world in efforts to preserve those rights and liberties. We give thanks for all those across the world who have joined with America in our fight against terrorism. We give thanks for the men and women of our military, who are fighting to defend our Nation and the future of civilization.

We continue to remember those who are suffering and face hardships. We pray for peace throughout the world.

On this National Day of Prayer, I encourage Americans to remember the words of St. Paul: "Do not be anxious about anything, but in everything, by prayer and petition, with thanksgiving, present your requests to God." The Congress, by Public Law 100-307, as amended, has called on our citizens to reaffirm the role of prayer in our society and to honor the religious diversity our freedom permits by recognizing annually a "National Day of Prayer."

NOW, THEREFORE, I, GEORGE W. BUSH, President of the United States of America, by virtue of the authority vested in me by the Constitution and law of the United States, do hereby proclaim May 2, 2002, as a National Day of Prayer. I ask Americans to pray for God's protection, to express gratitude of our blessing, and to seek moral and spiritual renewal. I urge all our citizens to join in observing this day with appropriate programs, ceremonies, and activities.

IN WITNESS WHEREOF, I have hereunto set my hand this twenty-sixth day of April, in the year of our Lord two thousand two, and of the Independence of the United States of America the two hundred and twenty-sixth.

—**George W. Bush**

Thanksgiving Day, 2002
By the President of the United States of America
A Proclamation Nov. 21, 2002

President Roosevelt's words gracefully reminds us that, as citizens of this great Nation, we have much for which to be thankful; and his timeless call inspires us to meet our responsibilities to help those in need and to promote greater understanding at home and abroad.

As the Pilgrims did almost four centuries ago, we gratefully give thanks this year for the beauty, abundance, and opportunity this great land offers. We also thank God for the importance of faith in our lives.

National Family Week, 2002
By the President of the United States of America
A Proclamation Nov. 24-30, 2002

Families provide a loving environment where children can flourish; and they help ensure that cultural traditions and timeless values are passed on to future generations. During National Family Week, we reaffirm the importance of families as a vital source of strength, confidence, and compassion for all of our citizens.

Strong families play a critical role in developing the character of our Nation. They teach children important standards of conduct such as accepting responsibility, respecting others and distinguishing the difference between right and wrong. By helping America's youth to grow into mature, thoughtful, and caring citizens, families help make our communities and our Nation safer and more civilized.

Raising a child requires sacrifice, commitment, and time; and we must expand our efforts to strengthen and empower families so that they can prepare children more effectively for the challenges of adulthood. We know that by helping couples to build and sustain strong, two-parent families, we will contribute to the well-being of our children and the strength of our society. Many single parents, grandparents, and others also raise their children in difficult circumstances, and these dedicated individuals deserve our respect and support.

As families come together to celebrate this Thanksgiving, I encourage every member of family in America to recognize the important role every other family member plays in making their lives whole and more complete. And as we give thanks for the love, commitment, and encouragement our families provide, we must recommit ourselves to strengthen our Nation by strengthening our families in ways that government never can.

National Days of Prayer and Remembrance Proclamation
Aug. 31th, 2002

As we remember the tragic events of September 11, 2001, and the thousands of innocent lives lost on that day, we recall as well the outpouring of compassion and faith that swept our Nation in the face of the evil done that day. In designating September 6-8 as National Days of Prayer and Remembrance, I ask all Americans to join together in cities, communities, neighborhoods, and places of worship to honor those who were lost, to pray for those who grieve, and to give thanks to God's enduring blessing on our land. And let us, through prayer, seek the wisdom, patience, and strength to bring those responsible for the attacks to justice and to press for a world at peace.

For the families and friends of those who died, each new day has required new courage. Their perseverance has touched us deeply, and their noble character has brought us hope. We stand with them in faith, and we cherish with them the memory of those who perished.

In the aftermath of the attacks, the words of the Psalms brought comfort to many. We trust God always to be our refuge and our strength, an ever-present help in time of trouble. Believing that One greater than ourselves watches over our lives and over this Nation, we continue to place our trust in Him.

The events of September 11 altered our lives, the life of this Nation, and the world. Americans responded to terror with resolve and determination, first recovering, now rebuilding, and, at all times, committing ourselves to protecting our people and preserving our freedom. And we have found hope and healing in our faith, families, and friendships. As we confront the challenges before us, I ask you to join me during these Days of Prayer and Remembrance in praying for God's continued protection and for the strength to overcome great evil with even greater good.

Family Day, 2002
By the President of the United States of America
A Proclamation Sept. 23, 2002

America's character begins in the home, where children learn proper standards of conduct, principled values, and the importance of service. Families provide children the encouragement, support, and love they need to become confident, compassionate, and successful members of society. We must work together to promote and preserve the health and security of our families by upholding the timeless values that have sustained our society through history.

Recent events have reminded Americans of the blessing of family and friends, and of the importance of faith. As a Nation, we have a renewed dedication to our freedom, our country, and our principles. In homes, school, places of worship, the workplace, and civic and social organizations, we must continue to encourage responsibility, compassion and good citizenship.

Americans must also act to fight crime and drugs, and provide a safe and healthy environment for our children. We can begin by working to strengthen the bonds and improving communication between parents and children. Research done by the National Center on Addiction and Substance Abuse at Columbia University has consistently showed that the more often children eat dinner with their parents, the less likely children are to smoke, drink, or use illegal drugs. Naturally, parents should be the most prominent and active figures in their children's lives. By spending more family time together, parents can better engage with their children and encourage them to make the right choices.

The nurturing and development of our families require investment, focus, and commitment. Strong families make strong and drug-free communities. By taking time to develop positive and open relationships with their children, parents help fight the war on drugs and encourage positive choices. Across our land, citizens, schools, and civic institutions can assist families by helping to meet the needs of all those who live in our communities. As we work together to strengthen our families, we will build a Nation of hope and opportunity for all.

Father's Day, 2002
By the President of the United States of America
A Proclamation June 14th, 2002

Fathers play a unique and important role in the lives of their children. As mentor, protector, and provider, a father fundamentally influences the shape and direction of his child's character by giving love, care, discipline, and guidance.

As we observe Father's Day, our Nation honors fatherhood and urges fathers to commit themselves selflessly to the success and well-being of ther children. And we reaffirm the importance of fathers in the lives of their children.

Raising a child requires significant time, effort, and sacrifice; and it is one of the most hopeful and fulfilling experiences a man can ever know. A father can derive great joy from seeing his child grow from infancy to adulthood. A a child matures into independence and self reliance, the value fo a parent's hard work, love, and commitment comes to fruition.

Responsible fatherhood is important to a healthy and civil society. Numerous studies comfirm that children whose fathers are present and involved in their lives are more likey to develop into prosperous and healthy adults. Children learn by example; and they need the father's presence as examples of virtue in their daily lives. A child's sense of security can be greatly enhanced by seeing his parents in a living and faithful marriage.

My Administration strongly supports initiatives to strengthen fatherhood, promote stable families, and increase the ease of adoptions. We must also continue to enlist the help of citizens and community groups who reach out to father-less or neglected chilren though mentoring and other acts of compassion.

8
Excerpts from George Washington's Farewell Address*

* Considered by many to be the greatest American political speech ever; was the object of study in American history for almost 200 years.

After mentioning that he plans to resign from office, a decision reached with "mature reflection" for the best interests of all, he prayed:

"that Heaven may continue to you the choicest tokens of its beneficence, that your union and brotherly affection may be perpetual; that the free Constitution which is the work of your hands may be sacredly maintained; that its administration in every department may be stamped with wisdom and virtue; that, in time, the happiness of the people of these States, under the auspices of liberty, may be made complete by so careful a preservation and so prudent a use of this blessing as will acquire to them the glory of recommending it to the applause, the affection, and adoption of every nation which is yet a stranger to it."

He then went on to recommend "some sentiments that are the result of much reflection . . . which appear to be all-important to the permanency of your felicity as a people." First and most importantly, he called for unity in government.

Most Commanding Motive — Unity of the Whole

"But these considerations, however powerfully they address themselves to your sensibility, are greatly outweighed by those which apply more immediately to your interest. Here, every portion of our country finds the most commanding motives for carefully guarding and preserving the union of the whole."

After stating that north, south, east and west sections of the country must all depend upon each other, he stated:

All United for Greater Strength

"While, then, every part of our country thus feels an immediate and particular interest in union, all the parts combined in the united mass of means and efforts cannot fail to find greater strength, greater resource, proportionately greater security from external danger . . . To the efficacy and permanency of your union, a government for the whole is indispensable. No alliances, however strict, between the parts can be an adequate substitute."

Constitution Cannot be Changed Without Consent of All

"But the constitution which at any time exists till changed by an explicit and authentic act of the whole people is sacredly obligatory upon all. The very idea of the power and the right of the people to establish government presupposes the duty of every individual to obey the established government."

Let No One Subvert Power of the People

"However combinations or associations of the above description may now and then answer popular ends, they are likely in the course of time and things to become potent engines by which cunning, ambitious, and unprincipled men will be enabled to subvert the power of the people, and to usurp for themselves the reins of government, destroying afterwards the very engines which have lifted them to unjust dominion."

Liberty with Properly Distributed Powers

"Liberty itself will find in such a government, with powers properly distributed and adjusted, its surest Guardian. It is, indeed, little else than a name where the Government is too feeble to withstand the enterprises of faction, to confine each member of the society within the limits prescribed by the laws, and to maintain all in the secure and tranquil enjoyment of the rights of person and property."

Strong Warning Against Spirit of Party

"I have already intimated to you the danger of parties in the State, with particular reference to the founding of them on geographical discriminations. Let me now take a more comprehensive view, and warn you in the most solemn manner against the baneful effects of the spirit of party generally.

"This Spirit, unfortunately, is inseparable from our nature, having its root in the strongest passions of the human mind. It exists under different shapes in all governments, more or less stifled, controlled, or repressed; but in those of the popular form it is seen in its greatest rankness and is truly their worst enemy."

Leads to Depotism

"The alternate domination of one faction over another, sharpened by the spirit of revenge natural to party dissension, which in different ages and countries has perpetrated the most horrid enormities, is itself a frightful despotism. But this leads at length to a more formal and permanent despotism. The disorders and miseries which result gradually incline the minds of men to seek security and repose in the absolute power of an individual, and sooner or later the chief of some prevailing faction, more able or more fortunate than his competitors, turns this disposition to the purposes of his own elevation on the ruins of public liberty."

Party Spirit is Harmful

"There is an opinion that parties in free countries are useful checks upon the administration of the government, and serve to keep alive the spirit of liberty. This within certain limits is probably true and in governments of a monarchical cast patriotism may look with indulgence, if not with favor, upon the spirit of party. But in those of the popular character, in governments purely elective, it is a spirit not to be encouraged. From their natural tendency it is certain there will always be enough of that spirit for every salutary purpose; and there being constant danger of excess, the effort ought to be by force of public opinion to mitigate and assuage it."

Uniform Vigilance

"A fire not to be quenched, it demands a uniform vigilance to prevent its bursting into a flame, lest, instead of warming, it should consume. It is important, likewise, that the habits of thinking in a free country should inspire caution in those entrusted with its administration to confine themselves within their respective constitutional spheres, avoiding in the exercise of the powers of one department to encroach upon another. The spirit of encroachment tends to consolidate the powers of all the departments in one, and thus to create, whatever the form of government, a real despotism. A just estimate of that love of power and proneness to abuse it which predominates in the human heart is sufficient to satisfy us of the truth of this position."

The Necessity of Reciprocal Checks

"The necessity of reciprocal checks in the exercise of political power, by dividing and distributing it into different depositories, and constituting each the guardian of the public weal against invasions by the others, has been evinced by experiments ancient and modern, some of them in our country and under our own eyes."

Distribution of Powers

"To preserve them must be as necessary as to institute them. If, in the opinion of the people, the distribution or modification of the constitutional powers be in any particular wrong, let it be corrected by an amendment in the way which the Constitution designates. But let there be no change by usurpation; for though this in one instance may be the instrument of good, it is the customary weapon by which free governments are destroyed. The precedent must always greatly overbalance in permanent evil any partial or transient benefit which their use can at any time yield."

Twin Pillars — Religion and Morality

"Of all the dispositions and habits which lead to political prosperity, religion and morality are indispensable supports."

Separation of God from State — UnAmerican

"In vain would that man claim the tribute of patriotism who should labor to subvert these great pillars of human happiness—these firmest props of the duties of men and citizens. The mere politician, equally with the pious man, ought to respect and to cherish them. A volume could not trace all their connections with private and public felicity. Let it simply be asked, "where is the security for property, for reputation, for life, if the sense of religious obligation desert the oaths which are the instruments of investigation in courts of justice?" And let us with caution indulge the supposition that morality can be maintained without religion. Whatever may be conceded to the influence of refined education on minds of peculiar structure, reason and experience both forbid us to expect that national morality can prevail in exclusion of religious principle."

Virtue Is a Necessary Spring of Popular Government

"It is substantially true that virtue or morality is a necessary spring of popular government. The rule indeed extends with more or less force to every species of free government. Who, that is a sincere friend to it, can look with indifference upon attempts to shake the foundation of the fabric?"

Public Opinion Should be Enlightened by Truth and Morality

"Promote, then, as an object of primary importance, institutions for the general diffusion of knowledge. In proportion as the structure of a government gives force to public opinion, it is essential that public opinion should be enlightened."

Cherish Public Credit

"As a very important source of strength and security, cherish public credit. One method of preserving it is to use it as sparingly as possible, avoiding occasions of expense by cultivating peace, but remembering also that timely disbursements to prepare for danger frequently prevent much greater disbursements to repel it; avoiding likewise the accumulation of debt, not only by shunning occasions of expense, but by vigorous exertions in times of peace to discharge the debts which unavoidable wars have occasioned, not ungenerously throwing upon posterity the burden which we ourselves ought to bear. The execution of these maxims belongs to your representatives; but it is necessary that public opinion should cooperate.

Taxes Necessary

"To facilitate to them the performance of their duty, it is essential that you should practically bear in mind that towards the payment of debts, there must be revenue; that to have revenue, there must be taxes; that no taxes can be devised which are not more or less inconvenient and unpleasant; that the intrinsic embarrassment, inseparable from the selection of the proper objects (which is always a choice of difficulties), ought to be a decisive motive for a candid construction of the conduct of the Government in making it, and for a spirit of acquiescence in the measures for obtaining revenue which the public exigencies may at any time dictate."

Good Faith and Justice Towards All Nations

"Observe good faith and justice towards all nations. Cultivate peace and harmony with all."

Religion and Morality Enjoin This Conduct

"Religion and morality enjoin this conduct. And can it be that good policy does not equally enjoin it? It will be worthy of a free, enlightened, and at no distant period a great nation to give to mankind the magnanimous and too novel example of a people always guided by an exalted justice and benevolence. Who can doubt that in the course of time and things the fruits of such a plan would richly repay any temporary advantages which might be lost by a steady adherence to it?"

God Oversees a Nation

"Can it be that Providence has not connected the permanent felicity of a nation with its virtue? The experiment, at least, is recommended by every sentiment which ennobles human nature."

Sin Will Destroy

"Alas! is it rendered impossible by its vices? In the execution of such a plan, nothing is more essential than that permanent, inveterate antipathies against particular nations and passionate attachments for others should be excluded, and that in place of them just and amicable feelings towards all should be cultivated."

Hatred Will Enslave

"The nation which indulges towards another an habitual hatred or an habitual fondness is in some degree a slave. It is a slave to its animosity or to its affection, either of which is sufficient to lead it astray from its duty and its interest. Antipathy in one nation against another disposes each more readily to offer insult and injury, to lay hold of slight causes of umbrage, and to be haughty and intractable when accidental or trifling occasions of dispute occur. Hence frequent collisions, obstinate, envenomed, and bloody contests."

Ill-Will Impels to War

"The nation prompted by ill-will and resentment sometimes impels to war the government contrary to the best calculations of policy. The government sometimes participates in the national propensity, and adopts through passion what reason would reject. At other times it makes the animosity of the nation subservient to projects of hostility, instigated by pride, ambition, and other sinister and pernicious motives. The peace often, sometimes perhaps the liberty, of nations has been the victim."

Favoritism Produces Evil

"So, likewise, a passionate attachment of one nation for another produces a variety of evils. Sympathy for the favorite nation, facilitating the illusion of an imaginary common interest in cases where no real common interest exists, and infusing into one enmities of the other, betrays the former into a participation in the quarrels and wars of the latter without adequate inducement or justification. It leads also to concessions to the favorite nation of privileges denied to others, which is apt doubly to injure the nation making the concessions by unnecessarily parting with what ought to have been retained, and by exciting jealousy, ill-will, and a disposition to retaliate in the parties from whom equal privileges are withheld; and it gives to ambitious, corrupted, or deluded citizens (who devote themselves to the favorite nation) facility to betray or sacrifice the interests of their own country without odium, sometimes even with popularity, gilding with the appearances of a virtuous sense of obligation, a commendable deference for public opinion, or a laudable zeal for public good the base or foolish compliances of ambition, corruption, or infatuation."

Warning Against Seduction

"As avenues to foreign influence in innumerable ways, such attachments are particularly alarming to the truly enlightened and independent patriot. How many opportunities do they afford to tamper with domestic factions, to practise the arts of seduction, to mislead public opinion, to influence or awe the public councils! Such an attachment of a small or weak nation toward a great and powerful nation dooms the former to be the satellite of the latter. Against the insidious wiles of foreign influence (I conjure you to believe me, fellow-citizens), the jealousy of a free people ought to be constantly awake, since history and experience prove that foreign influence is one of the most baneful foes of republican government. But that jealousy, to be useful, must be impartial, else it becomes the instrument of the very influence to be avoided, instead of a defense against it. Excessive partiality for one foreign nation and excessive dislike of another cause those whom they actuate to see danger only on one side, and serve to veil and even second the arts of influence on the other. Real patriots who may resist the intrigues of the favorite are liable to become suspected and odious, while its tools and dupes usurp the applause and confidence of the people to surrender their interests."

The Great Rule: "With Perfect Good Faith"

"The great rule of conduct for us, in regard to foreign nations, is, in extending our commercial relations to have with them as little political connection as possible. So far as we have already formed engagements, let them be fulfilled with perfect good faith. Here let us stop."

The Politics of Europe Have Failed

"Europe has a set of primary interests which to us have none or a very remote relation. Hence she must be engaged in frequent controversies, the causes of which are essentially foreign to our concerns. Hence, therefore, it must be unwise in us to implicate ourselves by artificial ties in the ordinary vicissitudes of her politics or the ordinary combinations and collisions of her friendships or enmities."

We Must Pursue a Different Course

"Our detached and distant situation invites and enables us to pursue a different course. If we remain one people, under an efficient government, the period is not far off when we may defy material injury from external annoyance; when we may take such an attitude as will cause the neutrality we may at any time resolve upon to be scrupulously respected; when belligerent nations, under the impossibility of making acquisitions upon us, will not lightly hazard the giving us provocation; when we may choose peace or war, as our interest, guided by our justice, shall counsel."

No Interweaving of Destiny with Europe

"Why forgo the advantages of so peculiar a situation? Why quit our own to stand upon foreign ground? Why, by interweaving our destiny with that of any part of Europe, entangle our peace and prosperity in the toils of European ambition, rivalship, interest, humor, or caprice?"

Steer Clear of Foreign Alliances

"It is our true policy to steer clear of permanent alliances with any portion of the foreign world, so far, I mean, as we are now at liberty to do it; for let me not be understood as capable of patronizing infidelity to existing engagements. I hold the maxim no less applicable to public than to private affairs, that honesty is always the best policy. I repeat, therefore, let those engagements be observed in their genuine sense. But in my opinion, it is unnecessary and would be unwise to extend them. Taking care always to keep ourselves by suitable establishments on a respectable defensive posture, we may safely trust to temporary alliances for extraordinary emergencies."

Harmony with All Nations Recommended

"Harmony, liberal intercourse with all nations are recommended by policy, humanity, and interest. But even our commercial policy should hold an equal and impartial hand, neither seeking nor granting exclusive favors or preferences; consulting the natural course of things; diffusing and diversifying by gentle means the streams of commerce, but forcing nothing; establishing with powers so disposed, in order to give trade a stable course, to define the rights of our merchants, and to enable the Government to support them, conventional rules of intercourse, the best that present circumstances and mutual opinion will permit, but temporary and liable to be from time to time abandoned or varied as experience and circumstances shall dictate; constantly keeping in view that it is folly in one nation to look for disinterested favors from another; that it must pay with a portion of its independence for whatever it may accept under that character; that by such acceptance it may place itself in the condition of having given equivalents for nominal favors, and yet of being reproached with ingratitude for not giving more. There can be no greater error than to expect or calculate upon real favors from nation to nation. It is an illusion which experience must cure, which a just pride ought to discard."

The Counsels of an Old and Affectionate Friend

"In offering to you, my countrymen, these counsels of an old and affectionate friend I dare not hope they will make the strong and lasting impression I could wish—that they will control the usual current of the passions or prevent our nation from running the course which has hitherto marked the destiny of nations. But if I may even flatter myself that they may be productive of some partial benefit, some occasional good—that they may now and then recur to moderate the fury of party spirit, to warn against the mischiefs of foreign intrigue, to guard against the impostures of pretended patriotism—this hope will be a full recompense for the solicitude for your welfare by which they have been dictated.

"How far in the discharge of my official duties I have been guided by the principles which have been delineated, the public records and other evidences of my conduct must witness to you and to the world. To myself, the assurance of my own conscience is that I have at least believed myself to be guided by them."

My Proclamation of April 22nd

"In relation to the still subsisting war in Europe my proclamation of the 22d of April, 1793, is the index to my plan. Sanctioned by your approving voice and by that of your representatives in both Houses of Congress, the spirit of that measure has continually governed me, uninfluenced by any attempts to deter or divert me from it."

A Neutral Position

"After deliberate examination, with the aid of the best lights I could obtain, I was well satisfied that our country, under all the circumstances of the case, had a right to take, and was bound in duty and interest to take, a neutral position. Having taken it, I determined as far as should depend upon me to maintain it with moderation, perseverance and firmness.

"The considerations which respect the right to hold this conduct, it is not necessary on this occasion to detail. I will only observe, that, according to my understanding of the matter, that right, so far from being denied by any of the belligerent powers, has been virtually admitted by all."

An Obligation of Justice

"The duty of holding a neutral conduct may be inferred, without any thing more, from the obligation which justice and humanity impose on every nation, in cases in which it is free to act, to maintain inviolate the relations of peace and amity towards other nations.

"The inducements of interest for observing that conduct will best be referred to your own reflections and experience. With me a predominant motive has been to endeavor to gain time for our country to settle and mature its yet recent institutions, and to progress without interruption to that degree of strength and consistency which is necessary to give it, humanly speaking, the command of its own fortunes."

Unconscious of Intentional Error, But Sensitive to My Defects

"Though, in reviewing the incidents of my Administration, I am unconscious of intentional error, I am nevertheless too sensible of my defects not to think it probable that I may have committed many errors."

A Fervent Prayer

"Whatever they may be, I fervently beseech the Almighty to avert or mitigate the evils to which they may tend. I shall also carry with me the hope that my country will never cease to view them with indulgence, and that, after forty-five years of my life dedicated to its service with an upright zeal, the faults of incompetent abilities will be consigned to oblivion, as myself must soon be to the mansions of rest."

A Fervent Love for My Country

"Relying on its kindness in this as in other things, and actuated by that fervent love toward it which is so natural to a man who views in it the native soil of himself and his progenitors for several generations, I anticipate with pleasing expectation that retreat in which I promise myself to realize without alloy the sweet enjoyment of partaking in the midst of my fellow citizens the benign influence of good laws under a free government—the ever-favorite object of my heart, and the happy reward, as I trust, of our mutual cares, labors, and dangers."

9
The Founding Fathers' Religious View of Education

American Education And The Founding Fathers

Judaic-Christianity was without doubt the foundation of the American educational system as envisioned by our Founding Fathers. It had been, in fact, for nearly a century and a half before 1776. The first education laws had been constructed upon Christian principles in the early 1600s. In 1642, the early settlers passed "The Old Deluder Satan Act" to make sure that the Bible would be the basis of our American system. This scripture-centered approach was universally accepted.

The New England Primer

The New England Primer, mentioned earlier, introduced in Boston in 1690 by Benjamin Harris, was the first textbook in America. For 100 years after its introduction, it was the beginning textbook for students. Until 1900 it continued to be the principal text in public, private, home and parochial schools. The Founders, as well as most other Americans, learned from it. In it were contained the Bible alphabet, Bible questions and the Shorter Catechism. The Bible was the other official textbook.

The value of the Shorter Catechism, an inseparable part of the Primer, was explained in the 1843 reprint:

"Our Puritan Fathers brought the Shorter Catechism with them across the ocean and laid it on the same shelf with the family Bible. They taught it diligently to their children If in this Catechism the true and fundamental doctrines of the Gospel are expressed in fewer and better words and definitions than in any other summary, why ought we not now to train up a child in the way he should go? — why not now put him in possession of the richest treasure that ever human wisdom and industry accumulated to draw from?"

The 1900 reprint described the impact of the Primer:

"The New England Primer was one of the greatest books ever published. It went through innumerable editions; it reflected in a marvelous way the spirit of the age that produced it, and contributed, perhaps more than any other book except the Bible, to the molding of those sturdy generations that gave to America its liberty and its institutions."

1991 Edition

The New England Primer was re-printed in 1991 by WallBuilders. David Barton and WallBuilders have done more to inform us of America's Godly heritage than any other group.

Christian Colleges

All the early colleges in this country were Christian including Harvard, Yale, William & Mary, Rutgers, and King's College. In 1860, for example, 262 of the then 288 college presidents as well as more than a third of all faculty members were ministers of the Gospel.

Harvard

Harvard educated John Adams, John Hancock, Samuel Adams,

and other Founding Fathers. Its educational purpose was clear: "Let every student be plainly instructed and earnestly pressed to consider well the main end of his life and studies is to know God and Jesus which is eternal life, John 17:3, and therefore to lay Christ in the bottom as the only foundation of all sound knowledge and learning." To help students attain this general goal, Harvard instituted specific practices. For example: "Everyone shall so exercise himself in reading the Scriptures twice a day that he shall be ready to give such an account of his proficiency therein." Each student was required to go to chapel service, to know and study the scriptures, and to live a moral life.

Yale (Founded 1699)

Yale is the school that educated Noah Webster, William Livingston, William Samuel Johnson and other prominent Founders. In 1720 Yale charged its students: "Seeing God is the giver of all wisdom, every scholar, besides private or secret prayer where in all we are bound to ask wisdom, shall be present morning and evening at public prayer. . ." Then in 1755 Yale students were instructed: "Above all have an eye to the great end of all your studies, which is to obtain the clearest conceptions of Divine things and to lead you to a saving knowledge of God in his Son Jesus Christ." Its 1787 rules declared: "All the scholars are required to live a religious and blameless life according to the rules of God's Word, diligently reading the holy Scriptures, that fountain of Divine light and truth, and constantly attending all the duties of religion. . . All the scholars are obliged to attend Divine worship in the College Chapel on the Lord's Day and on Days of Fasting and Thanksgiving appointed by public Authority."

Princeton

Princeton (a seminary for the training of ministers) educated more Founding Fathers than any other school—more than 200 of them including signers, James Madison, Richard Stockton, Benjamin Rush, Gunning Bedford, Jonathon Dayton, as well as JohnWitherspoon Its first president declared, "Cursed be all that learning that is contrary to the cross of Christ!" Notice some of

Princeton's requirements while John Witherspoon was president: "Every student shall attend worship in the college hall morning and evening at the hours appointed and shall behave with gravity and reverence during the whole service. Every student shall attend public worship on the Sabbath. . .Besides the public exercises of religious worship on the Sabbath, there shall be assigned to each class certain exercises for their religious instruction suited to the age and standing of the pupils. . .and no student belonging to any class shall neglect them."

Dartmouth

In 1754, Dartmouth College of New Hampshire (made especially famous by alumnus Daniel Webster's defense of its charter before the U.S. Supreme Court in 1819) was founded by the Rev. Eleazar Wheelock. Its charter was very succinct as to its purpose: "Whereas. . .the Reverend Eleazar Wheelock. . .educated a number of the children of the Indian natives with a view to their carrying the Gospel in their own language and spreading the knowledge of the great Redeemer among their savage tribes. And. . .the design became reputable among the Indians insomuch that a larger number desired the education of their children in said school. . . [Therefore] Dartmouth-College [is established] for the education and instruction of youths. . .in reading, writing and all parts of learning which shall appear necessary and expedient for civilizing and Christianizing the children."

Columbia

Columbia College, founded in 1754, had as its first president William Samuel Johnson. Its admission requirements stated: "No candidate shall be admitted into the College. . .unless he shall be able to render into English. . .the Gospels from the Greek. . .It is also expected that all students attend public worship on Sundays." Johnson's commencement speech was powerful. He stated: "You this day, gentlemen,. . .have. . .received a public education, the purpose whereof hath been to qualify you the better to serve your Creator and your country. . .Your first great duties, you are sensible, are those you owe to Heaven, to your Creator and Redeemer.

Let these be ever present to your minds and exemplified in your lives and conduct. Imprint deep upon your minds the principles of piety towards God and a reverence and fear of His holy name. The fear of God is the beginning of wisdom. . .Remember, too, that you are the redeemed of the Lord, that you are bought with a price, even the inestimable price of the precious blood of the Son of God . . .Love, fear, and serve Him as your Creator, Redeemer, and Sanctifier. Acquaint yourselves with Him in His Word and holy ordinances. Make Him your friend and protector and your felicity is secured both here and hereafter."

Rutgers

Rutgers was founded in 1766 by Reverend Theodore Frelinghuysen. Rutgers also had the same Christian ideals and the insistence upon chapel visit, Bible reading, and the Christian moral code.

George Washington

The Founder of our country provided the most succinct description of America's education philosophy when he stated: "You do well to wish to learn our arts and ways of life, and above all, the religion of Jesus Christ. These will make you a greater and happier people than you are. Congress will do every thing they can to assist you in this wise intention." He said this to chiefs from the Delaware Indian tribe who had brought him three Indian youths to be trained in American schools. He further stated: "Congress. . . will look upon them as their own children."

The Tradition Carries On

A school in Philadelphia in 1844 petitioned that it be allowed to teach morality but not religion. The case came before the Supreme Court which responded in this way: "Why may not the Bible, and especially the New Testament. . .be read and taught as a divine revelation in the [school]—its general precepts expounded. . .and its glorious principles of morality inculcated?. . . Where can the purest principles of morality be learned so clearly or so perfectly as from the New Testament?"

From 1776 To 1962

The Judaic-Christian Foundation of America's schools persisted until 1962 when five members of our Supreme Court did something that was completely unconstitutional. Our Constitution clearly states that Congress should make no laws prohibiting the free exercise of religion. For the first time in American history it forbade public school teachers, administrators and students to pray in public schools. At the time of the law, 97% of all Americans disagreed with this decision. It was completely un-American and definitely unconstitutional, for we were a nation under God. Since that fateful day, public school education has steadily declined. In category after category, negative and immoral behavior in public school students has escalated and the SAT scores have steadily declined. Now on an average, they're more than 100 points lower than they were in 1962. David Barton of WallBuilders has charts after charts showing this in his book *To Pray Or Not To Pray*.

American Education On The Decline

Since 1962, American education has been on the decline. Books like *Why Johnny Can't Read* and *Why Johnny Can't Tell Right From Wrong* are bestsellers. We now use the word "meltdown" to describe the education system in most major cities. Before the pilgrims landed, they signed the Mayflower Contract in which they stated they would create an educational system so that their children could read and learn the Scriptures. Today that is virtually the only book censored in American public school classrooms. William Holmes McGuffey, author of *The New England Primer*, also wrote *McGuffey's Eclectic Reader* which sold 120 million copies. Along with the Bible and *The New England Primer* it provided the backbone for grammar school education in this country. In that reader, McGuffey stated: "The Ten Commandments and the teachings of Jesus Christ are not only basic but plenary." Today McGuffey's *Readers* are outlawed.

State Education

In the 19th century, state education came into existence. This public education was paid for by tax dollars with laws requiring the education of children. Slowly private academies and Christian schools began to go out of existence. Our public school educational system began to be more secular.

The Twentieth Century

In the 20th century, things got worse. Modern progressive education was introduced and spread across the country. The great architect of this new movement was John Dewey. Columbia Teacher's College, where he taught, trained thousands of teachers. Dewey brought about what is called a Copernican revolution putting man rather than God at its center. Thus humanism gradually became the ideology of our public school system. Dewey was one of the signers of this humanist manifesto which stated: "No Diety will save us, we will save ourselves."

Everything In State Of Flux

One of the inevitable results of this atheistic humanism was the demise of all objective and eternal standards of truth and morality. In the minds of Humanists there are no eternal truths, all is relative. All is changing. Everything is in a state of flux with no eternal verities and no objective moral standards. Dewey and the Humanists were rebels against religion.

Results Of The Revolution

Dr. W. P. Shofstall, state Superintendent for public schools in Arizona stated: "The Atheists have, for all practical purposes, taken over public education in this country." Values clarification has replaced moral absolutes. The Ten Commandments have been replaced. Every student is taught that it's up to them to decide what is right and what is wrong. The results have been an ever increasing number of "Littletons". The prophesy of the Bible has been fulfilled. "Every man did that which was right in his own eyes." Chaos rules the schools. Today we are mass producing highly materialistic, hedonistic and self-centered youth. Instead of Godly teachers we now have policeman in the classrooms. Muggings, robberies, rapes, and murders among high school youngsters have escalated in a most frightening way. Drug use is endemic. Alcoholism is rampant. Promiscuity is everywhere. The two major causes for death among college students are suicide and murder. High school pregnancies, abortions and VD are escalating problems. Sex education is not based upon moral standards but on the philosophy of Planned Parenthood which endorses both heterosexual and homosexual activity. No moral standards are set.

The Promise Of America

One series of social studies textbooks is called *The Promise of America*. A mother spoke to the teacher about it and became alarmed when the teacher said: "We don't show some textbooks to parents." When the children went out to recess she borrowed her son's textbook. It was filled with profanity, blasphemies and obscenities. It endorsed illicit sex, homosexuality and abortion. It dragged the Church and God in the mud and was highly unpatriotic.

Rise Of Christian Schools

Because of the tremendous problem in public schools, there has been a rise in attendance at Christian schools. Home schooling is also on the rise. Right now by far the majority of Americans want God, prayer, family values, and the Ten Commandments to be taught in public schools. Since September 11, over 300,000 "In God We Trust" posters are back in public schools. When public school children imitated their parents and elected officials by singing God Bless America, the American Civil Liberties (ACLU) protested. This caused a member of the House of Representatives to introduce a new law allowing God Bless America to be sung in public schools. It passed the House of Representatives 404 to 0. Years ago, Martin Luther stated: "I am much afraid that schools will prove to be great gates of hell unless they diligently labor in explaining the Holy Scriptures, engraving them in the hearts of youth. I advise no one to place his child where the Scriptures do not reign paramount. Every institution in which men are not increasingly occupied with the word of God must become corrupt."

The Revival of Our Nation
What our country needs now more than ever is a revival as we had during the great awakenings of the 1800s.

Up or Down
Again, the question of the hour for our students, teachers and school is: "Which way are we to go? Up with God and morality, or further down into the absolute meltdown of wisdom and morals?"

10
12 Principles that Made America Great

Eternal Rules of Order

Our first president, George Washington, stated in his first inaugural address, "The propitious smiles of heaven can never be expected on a nation that disregards the eternal rules of order and right that heaven itself has ordained." What are these eternal rules of order ordained by heaven itself that made the United States so great?

America became a great nation not because she had a wealth of natural resources or a population of intellectual giants. America became great because, as a country, we adhered to those eternal rules of order and right which heaven, itself, had ordained.

I. A Nation Under God
The first principle, therefore, is that we were a nation under God. Our founding fathers explicitly founded this nation as a nation under God. They took a positive and definitive stand for God and for the Bible. They founded this nation upon the laws of nature (the natural law) and the laws of nature's God (the Bible). That was the bedrock foundation of this country. That was the rock upon which our nation was built. We were a God-fearing people.

II. Unalienable Right To Life

The second principle upon which we were founded was the God-given, inalienable dignity and right to life of every American citizen. (As a nation, "we hold these truths to be self-evident that all men are endowed by their Creator with certain inalienable rights," the first of which is the right to life, then liberty and the pursuit of happiness.) The dignity of the human person is foundational in the American political scheme. Our Founding Fathers realized that this dignity was not granted by the state or by a dictator or even by the vote of the people. It was the dignity given from above by God Himself.

This dignity was so ingrained in each American citizen that it was also inalienable. In other words, this dignity could not be subverted, denied or taken away by any force on earth; not by the president nor even by the Supreme Court. This God-given, inalienable dignity was so clearly taught that it was considered self-evident. In short, even if you had not read the Bible or ever heard a sermon, you would know it intuitively. It was that clear that every single American citizen had the right to his dignity and the right to life and freedom, as well.

III. Ordered Freedom

The third principle was the principle of liberty. Our history was one of freedom, but freedom ordered to the laws of nature and the laws of nature's God. Our sounding cry is 'liberty and justice for all!' We could not be forced to accept religious, political or economic oppression. We were to be a free people. Even slavery was considered as un-American. So important was this to the American people, that we fought the Civil War to assure every citizen that they had the right to freedom.

IV. Traditional Family

The fourth principle was the principle of the traditional monogamous family. Because America was founded upon the Judaic-Christian ethic, as a nation we were pro-family and, even more so, for the traditional monogamous family. As a nation, we believed that marriage was between one man and one woman fully entered into for the procreation and education of children for life. As a nation, we respected the awesome dignity of marriage, womanhood and sexuality. Sodomy and pornography, therefore, were outlawed in this country right from our inception, as were divorce and the oppression of women.

V. Common Decency

The fifth principle was the principle of common decency. Flowing from the previous principle of respect for traditional family life, is the principle of common decency. Not only was pornography outlawed throughout the land but vulgarity in the open forum was outlawed, as well. Proper dress was always modest.

VI. A Solid Work Ethic

The sixth principle is that of a Judaic-Christian work ethic. As a people, we realized that we were to work in union with God on the ongoing creation of the world. America was founded upon the dignity of hard work. Our free enterprise system encouraged ambition, incentive and competition, as well as, blood, sweat and tears.

VII. A God Ordained Covenant

The seventh principle is the principle of covenant. As a people raised with a proper understanding of God's covenant, we realized that we were working in union with Him. "I will be your God and you will be my people." We trusted in His divine providence. Or, as John F. Kennedy expressed it (and quoted previously in this work), "Let us go forward with God's blessing but realizing that, here on earth, God's work must truly be our own." (Inaugural Address).

VIII. God Centered Education

The eighth principle is the principle of God-centered education. Just as the Bible and the *New England primer* were the official textbooks throughout our land, all education was to be God-centered. The first colleges in this country were Christian and every student had to do at least these three things: to attend chapel service on Sunday, to read the Bible and say their prayers every day, and to practice the Judaic-Christian moral code.

IX. Divinely Ordained Homes

The ninth principle is the principle of divinely ordained establishments. The first of these divinely-ordained establishments was the home. The home was always considered the basic unit of our society. Our Founding Fathers realized that our country would only be as strong as the home where mothers and fathers not only loved each other, but truly loved their children and where children, in return, truly respected, loved and honored their parents. Parental responsibility was supreme and all teachers would teach in the place of parents themselves.

X. Divinely Ordained State

The tenth principle is the second divinely ordained establishment which is the state. As a people, we were taught to respect civil authority and to pray for our leaders. We were also strongly encouraged to elect righteous men; and we were strongly warned over and again that if we did not do so, catastrophe would follow. William Penn, for example, said, quoting Proverbs 29:2, "When the righteous rule, the people rejoice; when the wicked rule, the people roam." Noah Webster stated, "When you become entitled to exercise the right of voting for public officers, let it be impressed on your mind that God commands you to choose for rulers, 'just men who will rule in the fear of God.' The preservation of [our] government depends on the faithful discharge of this duty. If the citizens neglect their duty and place unprincipled men in office, the government will soon be corrupted; laws will be made, not for the public good so much as for selfish or local purposes; corrupt or incompetent men will be appointed to execute the laws; the public revenues will be squandered on unworthy men; and the rights of the citizens will be violated or disregarded."

XI. A National Respect For The Church

The eleventh principle is based on the third divinely ordained establishment which was the church. Our Founding Fathers clearly wanted the Bible to be the main source book of our government. Blackstone's commentary on the law read like a Bible. "Our laws reflect the teaching s of Jesus." (Supreme Court, 1892)

XII. Freedom Of Religion

The twelfth principle is freedom of religion. The primary purpose of the establishment of the United States was freedom of religion. Every American citizen was free to express their own religious conviction.

These 12 principles made America great. These principles were expressed in Samuel Rutherford's *Lex, Rex.* "Unlike the governments of Europe that assured the divine right of kings, all men in America, even our rulers, were to be under the law of God as revealed through the Scriptures and not above it." Though Rutherford died before his concepts were implemented, his principles lived on. John Witherspoon brought these principles into the Constitution. The renowned jurist, William Blackstone, embodied the tenents of Judaic-Christian theism in his commentaries. These commentaries were not merely an approach to the study of our laws but, for most lawyers, they constituted all there was of our law. Blackstone, a Christian, believed that the fear of the Lord was the beginning of wisdom, thus he opened his commentaries with a careful analysis of the law of God as revealed in the Scriptures. He took it as self-evident that God is the source of all laws, whether they were found in the Scriptures or observable in nature. His presuppositions were thoroughly Christian, founded upon the belief that there was an Almighty God who personally governed in the affairs of men. And as a consequence, Americans were bound by those laws as they were to other absolutes. Blackstone's influence is clearly expressed in the Declaration of Independence where it speaks of 'the laws of nature and the laws of nature's God'.

The Bible

John Quincy Adams would say, "The first and almost only book deserving of universal attention is the Bible."

11
Major Trends Affecting The Catholic Church

Influenced by the Reformation
The Catholic Church started in America during the time of the Reformation. Christianity was divided in Europe. That had tremendous impact upon Christianity in America although Christopher Columbus, Vasco Da Gama, Father Junipero Serra, Amerigo Vespucci, Marquette and many of the early explorers were Catholic. Non-Catholic Christians poured into America, as well.

Founding Fathers Were Christians
The founding fathers therefore, were mostly non-Catholic Evangelical Christians, and they set this nation upon a tripod (1) the laws of Nature, (2) the Bible, and (3) a God-given inalienable dignity and right to life of every citizen. We were a nation not only under God, but under Christ.

Catholic-Protestant Tension
There has always been tension between Catholics and Protestants in this country. In the 1890's for example, Irish farmers literally protected their churches from burning with pitchforks.

Rise of Communism
In 1917, our Blessed Mother warned us that if we did not return to her Son, there would be the rise of an atheistic system known as Communism and also a second world war, worse than the first. That war began for us Americans on her feast day, December 8, 1941 and ended on her feast day August 15, 1945. Many social changes in American life happened because of the war. With it, began the first wave of a permissive sexual revolution.

The Golden Age of Modern American Catholicism
During the cold war, Catholicism entered a golden age. Movies, for example, portrayed the Church and the priesthood and the sisters in a glowing way. For three consecutive years (1943, 1944, 1945), "Song of Bernadette, " "Going My Way," "The Bells of St.

Mary's, and "The Keys of the Kingdom" were nominated for 34 Oscars and won 12. Spencer Tracy as Father Flannagan of "Boy's Town," Bing Crosby as Fr. Chuck O'Malley in "Going My Way," Karl Malden, as a labor priest in "On the Waterfront," William Gargan as a compassionate priest in "You Only Live Once" and Pat O'Brien in "San Francisco" produced the image of the priest as wise, manly, good-humored, and compassionate.

There was not a single World War II movie where the battle-field chaplain was not a Catholic priest. Bishop Fulton Sheen, with a peak audience of 30 million, was the darling of radio and television. Father Keller of The Christophers ("It is better to light one candle.") and Father Patrick Payton with his Rosary Crusades, ("The family that prays together stays together.") enhanced the image of the Church and many Catholic movie personalities appeared on television for them.

Prayer Removed from Public Schools

Beginning in the 1960s, with the explicit taking of prayer out of public schools, there began a great sociological decline. Within a generation, we saw the rise of the Rock 'n' Roll, and the infamous Roe v. Wade decision that ushered abortion on demand into our culture, and secular humanism became the new religion of the media.

Influence of the Vietnam War

With the Vietnam War, Woodstock and the rise of the rock and roll era there was a growing tendency to mistrust authority. The lies of Vietnam weakened respect for government. The distrust of government escalated with scandals in the military, of the FBI at Waco, and with the public admissions of greed and harassment of citizens by the IRS. It was evident in the overall disgust for the law, especially after the O.J. Simpson trial, and was further exacerbated by the shameless acts of the Clinton administration. There was a growing cynicism on the part of many women concerning the institution of marriage when the decline of morals on colleges campuses, divorce and abortion became prevalent.

Post Vatican II

The Catholic Church was also undermined as many Catholics spoke disdainfully of the "institutional Church." Criticism and dissent, especially after the Encyclical Humanae Vitae (concerning artificial birth control), scandals, pedophile priests, clergy resignations, and some well-publicized bad decisions, have added to the difficulties of the Church.

The Breakdown Of The Catholic Ghettos

Throughout this country there were Polish, German, Irish, Italian, and Slovak ghettos, where Catholics sent their children to parochial schools and jealously preserved their national customs — attending novenas and missions, holding processions, eating ethnic foods blessed by the priest, and honoring patron saints from their countries. Then people moved to the suburbs, and grandchildren were homogenized into secular Americans who no longer spoke the languages, kept the customs or went to Church.

Unfortunately, the media has become the new educator of American youth. Family is now fifth in influence and religion is seventeenth with the result that American Catholics, along with the general American population, have very liberal views concerning religion and morality. Most Americans recognize Mickey Mouse, McDonald's, Princess Di, Sylvester Stallone, Tom Cruise, Madonna, and Leonardo Di Caprio before they recognize the names of St. Theresa, St. John of the Cross, or St. Augustine. As a key influence, our American media has become dominated by owners and managers who are anti-religious, anti-Christian, anti-Catholic, anti-life and anti-family. Abortion on demand, widespread promiscuity and a rugged materialism and hedonism have daunted our print and broadcast media that now extends to the Internet.

The American entertainment industry has a virtual monopoly on the images that influence young people throughout the world. The omnipresence of the media with its secular gospel is so pervasive that it leaves little time for reflection and for a spiritual life. In recent polls, many Christians say the main significance of Christmas and Easter is that it is a time for families to get together. And how do many Christian children and grandchildren spend Holy

Week? The answer is Disneyland. In American culture today, Graceland replaces Lourdes, Disneyland replaces Church, and religious habits are replaced by jeans.

Widespread Diversity
With a smorgasbord of different values being offered, diversity becomes the "in" word. Since there are so many types of religious and spiritual experience out there, from New Age to Fundamentalism, the average American Christian falls into an unconscious relativism: One religion is as good as the next, and all religious experiences are pretty near equal. "Just as long as you believe in God."

The Success Of Evangelical Religion
In the past 50 years there has been a proliferation of other religions. There are over 2,000 different denominations in the United States, and nearly half were founded since 1965. The growth of Mormonism has been astounding as well as the growth of Jehovah's Witnesses, Assemblies of God and the Church of God in Christ. Many of these have claimed large numbers of former Catholics. Furthermore, the American landscape is no longer predominantly Christian. There are almost 1,000,000 Hindus in this Country compared with 70,000 twenty years ago. There are as many Muslims as there are Presbyterians and there are 750,000 Buddhists, the fastest growing Eastern religion in the United States. All this has led to a real relativism.

The Loss Of The Sacred Within The Churches
Many times traditional Christianity becomes so worldly it cannot serve the universal need for true searchers after the holy. Many ministers and priests have opted more for psychology than spirituality and moral categories are replaced by therapeutic ones. The sacred mindset has converted to secularism.

The Rise Of Religious Illiteracy
Most Catholics no longer know their faith. They have not been introduced to the Bible, and the Catechism is now "out of date."

Dislocation Following Vatican II

Liberal Catholics said the Council did not go far enough. Conservative Catholics said the council went too far.

Scandals that Rocked the Church

The most humbling event in modern American Catholic history is, of course, the priest sexual abuse scandals that hit the Church in 2002. Most infamous, of course, were those that rocked the archdiocese of Boston, where it was disclosed that about 80 priests in the last 40 years had been charged with pedophilia or homosexuality concerning youngsters. Two priests, Fr. John Geoghan and Fr. Paul Shanley were guilty of countless offenses. Cardinal Bernard Law was accused of negligence in reassigning them over and again to assignments where children were not protected. All this resulted in the American cardinals being called to Rome by Pope John Paul II for a special meeting.

Bishops Meeting

The bishops meeting in June of that year resolved that they would establish a national office for child and youth protection whose function would be to assist dioceses in the implementation of safe environment programs, assisting provinces and regions in the development of appropriate mechanisms to audit adherence to polices and to promote annually a public report on the progress made in the implementation of these standards.

Secondly, each diocese is to further establish safe environment programs, which would cooperate with parents, civil authorities, educators, and community organizations to provide a safe environment for all children.

Third, each diocese is to evaluate the background of all diocesan and parish personnel who have contact with children and would employ adequate screening techniques in deciding the fitness of candidates for ordination to the priesthood. Fourth, before giving any priest or deacon a new assignment, the bishop or major superior is to review a complete description of the cleric's record.

The bishops state, "We pledge most solemnly to one another and you, God's people, that we will work to our utmost for the protection of children and youth.

"We pledge that we will devote to this goal the resources and personnel necessary to accomplish it.

"We pledge that we will do our best to ordain to the priesthood and put into positions of trust only those who share this commitment to protecting children and youth.

"We pledge that we will work toward healing and reconciliation for those sexually abused by clerics.

"We make these pledges with a humbling sense of our own limitations and relying on the help of God and the support of his faithful priests and people to work with us to fulfill them.

"Above all we believe, in the words of St. Paul, cited by Pope John Paul II last April, 'where sin increased, grace overflowed all the more' (Rom 5:20). This is faith's message. With this faith, we are confident that we will not be conquered by evil but overcome evil with good" (cf Rom 12:21).

Section II
A Nation In Decay

12
The Great American Dream
Becomes a Hideous Nightmare

"Your young men shall dream dreams and your old men shall see visions" (Acts 2:17).

God Shed His Grace on Thee

Catherine Lee Bates wrote these immortal words "Oh beautiful for spacious skies, for amber waves of grain, for purple mountain majesties, above the fruited plain! America! America! God shed His grace on thee, and crown thy good with brotherhood from sea to shining sea!" Yes, God has blessed America like no other place on this planet Earth because America was founded and dedicated as a nation under God. God elevated our country from its infancy to a place of world leadership, allowing us to enjoy unprecedented goodness, development, freedom, and influence. America led the world in medical and technological advancements. This nation has pioneered in space, pushed back the frontiers of science and has given us the world's highest standard of living. We have opened our arms to millions of immigrants and refugees, first, from Europe and then from the Far East, and then from Latin America. For with grateful and humble hearts we honor the God who blessed us.

The Last Four Decades

From 1962 on, we began to attribute our blessings, not so much to God, but to ourselves. We have forgotten the warning of Lincoln:

"We have been the recipients of the choicest bounties of heaven. We have been preserved, these many years, in peace and prosperity. We have grown in numbers, wealth and power, as no other nation has ever grown. But we have forgotten God. We have forgotten the gracious hand which preserved us in peace, and multiplied and enriched and strengthened us; and we have vainly imagined, in the deceitfulness of our hearts, that all these blessings were produced by some superior wisdom and virtue of our own. Intoxicated with unbroken success, we have become too self-sufficient to feel the necessity of redeeming and preserving grace, too proud to pray to the God that made us! It behooves us, then to humble ourselves before the offended Power, to confess our national sins, and to pray for clemency and forgiveness." (April 30, 1863, Lincoln's Proclamation for a National Day of Fasting, Humiliation and Prayer.)

We have forgotten the power that has made and preserved us as a nation, as our national anthem says. We allowed secular humanism to infiltrate all of our institutions.

No System Under God

Each one of our systems has gone awry. The media system, the educational system, the medical system, the entertainment system, the political system, the economic system, the military system and, in many ways, even the religious system. The Ten Commandments no longer had the place of honor that our Founding Fathers gave them, and sin began to multiply. The first Commandment, a Nation under God has been replaced by separation of God and State. Blaspheming the name of God is now legal in every one of our states. The Third Commandment used to be protected by "blue laws." All of them have now been dismissed and Sunday is primarily a national day for sports.

We have violated the Fifth Commandment by killing over 100,000,000 babies. In addition, another murder occurs every 27 minutes in this country. The Sixth Commandment is violated openly by widespread sodomy, adultery, pornography, and promiscuity. Teenage pregnancies, incest and child abuse draw national attention and more than 2,000,000 Americans contract gonorrhea every year. And AIDS among this country's citizens is in epidemic proportions. Some two million unmarried couples now live together and the IRS has defined abortion clinics as "charitable" tax exempt organizations.

The Seventh Commandment is violated to the extent that a serious crime is committed every three seconds and a robbery every eighty seconds. There are now more than 9,000,000 alcoholics, 43,000,000 marijuana users, and half a million heroin addicts. America once legislated against all these things that God said were wrong, but gradually we began to tolerate all of the above, and the only virtue left was "tolerance" of evil. First we accepted these sins, then we justified them, then we condoned them, then we promoted them, then we legislated for them and then began to attack Christ and His Church, for speaking against them. Perversion and degradation that once made us blush, are now flaunted before the eyes of the nation that was conceived in the fear of the Lord. It happened little by little, not because someone forced it upon us, but because we have become indifferent.

Fear to Stand Up

So many Americans are afraid now to swim upstream. It takes courage to consistently speak out against those things that are harming us. Thank God for the remnant of Jews, Evangelicals, and Catholics who are holding the line. If they give way, our nation goes totally into decline.

The Underside of Capitalism

The Rise Of Corporate Capitalism. Whatever benefit capitalism has brought to our country, it cannot be denied it has done great harm to the fabric of the family and community. Many people were uprooted from their family backgrounds with the introduction of suburbia, and the high mobility that capitalism demands. Divorce and fragmentation of families spread. Furthermore, the success and complete dominance of world wide corporations have smothered local ethnic and religious groups. Although there are some good programming on television, in the end, both good and bad programs are identical in this respect: They are brought to us by companies trying to sell things. And materialism has become the new purpose of life.

Science "Contradicting" Religion

Modern science with its emphasis on evolution and its professed ability to explain away miracles became another serious challenge and the new technology cannot only clone animals but apparently, human babies as well.

A new psychology replaced spirituality making sin obsolete. Now accordingly there are only "early traumas", "road rage", "suppression", "victim-hood" and the "new adjustment therapy". Much of what was thought of as vice has even become virtue, and the overall goal of man is not a life laid down for others, but self-fulfillment.

Unfortunately, the media has been run in general by anti-religious, anti-Christian, anti-Catholic, anti-life and anti-family liberals. Abortion on demand, widespread promiscuity and a rugged materialism and hedonism have daunted our newspapers, television and even the internet.

Stemming the Tide

The main forces stemming the tide of such anti-American paganism have been conservative evangelicals and Jews. As John Leo stated in his excellent article "With Bias Towards All" (U.S. News and World Report, March 18, 2002), "There is a total disconnect between regular Americans who understand that the news is being packaged by leftist irreligious who consider anyone who doesn't agree with them 'a right wing nut'."

Bigotry Again Raises Its Ugly Head

When Hitler wanted to attack the Jews, he got the media to go along with him by printing that Jewish merchants were greedy money lenders and the like. Only the Catholic Church stood strong, as Albert Einstein so eloquently stated in *Time* Magazine, December 23, 1940:

"Being a lover of freedom, when the revolution came to Germany, I looked to the universities to defend it, knowing that they had always boasted of their devotion to the cause of truth; but no, the universities were immediately silenced. Then I looked to the great editors of the newspapers whose flaming editorials in days gone by had proclaimed their love of freedom, but they, like the universities, were silenced in a few short weeks. Only the Catholic

Church stood squarely across the path of Hitler's campaign toward suppressing the truth. I never had any special interest in the Catholic Church before, but now I feel a great affection and admiration because the Church alone has had the courage and persistence to stand for intellectual truths and moral freedom. I am forced thus to confess, that which I once despised I now praise unreservedly."

Let's Be Positive

Ironically, the newspapers across this nation are calling for a "No Tolerance" child abuse policy. What a wonderful ideal - one that should be embraced by everyone and by every organization. Our children are our greatest treasures. Each one of them is made to the image and likeness of God. Each one of them is a unique, incomparable, miracle and masterpiece of nature and grace. But each one of these precious children today are vulnerable to the onslaught of abuse that now surrounds them on every side. Each one is being easily victimized today by the almost un-American culture that is far too materialistic, hedonistic, pornographic, irreligious, and anti-life.

As Americans, we hold that each child is "endowed by their Creator" with "certain inalienable rights" — first, "to life", then to freedom and "liberty", and then to "the pursuit of happiness." The United Nations has an entire list of children's rights in its famous Magna Carta for children. To protect the innocence of our children, ten practical aims must be put in place right across the board.

1. First and foremost, we must bring this nation to be, once again, a nation under God, founded upon these 12 great principles that made America great. (see pg. 61)
2. "No tolerance" for abortion right across the board. Abortion has killed over 100 million of our children. (50 million surgically, 50 million through the "aborifacies pill.") Mother Teresa predicted that any nation that destroys children would be inflicted with war.
3. A "no tolerance policy" of pornography. Pornography has now become mainstream America. It infects most of our children. It is blatant in the music industry, in the entertainment industry, in

the movie industry; and many advertisements (including those in daily newspapers) can be classified as soft porn. Even in our sports pages are found ads offering children pornographic movies. Pornography now has invaded the Internet. No American child is free from its ugly influence. Pornography dehumanizes women, especially.

4. A "no tolerance" policy concerning sexual abuse. One out of every three girls is being sexually abused in the home, and apparently one out of every six boys. Outside the home, the highest offenders are homosexuals; followed by gynecologists and abortionists, where sexual abuse is apparently as high as 20 to 25 percent.

5. A "no tolerance" policy of offensive speech. On the one hand, we have sexual harassment laws; and on the other we allow people like Howard Stern and Jerry Springer and many of our movies to dehumanize people, especially, women, through highly degrading and offensive speech. Sexual harassment laws have been pushed and maintained for the sake of our children.

6. A "no tolerance" policy of sodomy. This is the sin that brought down Sodom and Gomorrah, and it's bringing down America; and it's wrong. There is nothing wrong with being a homosexual, but there is something very wrong with sodomy, especially as it affects children.

7. A "no tolerance" policy of public sexual education that treats children as if they were not sacred and sex as something that is devoid of sacredness and sublimity. Virginity should be taught to all of our children as a preparation for life and stable marriage.

8. A "no tolerance" policy on drugs, alcohol and nicotine. Drugs have been a scourge on the landscape of America, infesting our culture, and has led to dehumanizing behavior, suicide, and auto deaths. Alcohol, along with promiscuity, is the leading problem on our college campuses. And tobacco use, that often starts with young teenagers, has lead to early, meaningless death for countless millions of Americans.

9. A "no tolerance" policy of co-ed dorms where young people are exposed at very vulnerable ages to overwhelming temptations, to which most of them succumb.

10. A "no tolerance" policy to a media blitz that accentuates the negative, the violent, the offensive, the irreligious, the pagan, and the pornographic. Our newspapers should be held accountable to what is noblest in the minds and hearts of our children. Our children deserve this.

11. A "no tolerance" policy on violence, including the use of guns, knives, and violent objects. Littleton should have taught us all a lesson.

12. A "no tolerance" policy towards terrorism, either physical, mental or moral. Sept. 11 has taught us all a lesson.

Only when everyone takes child abuse seriously will it stop. Our children are being victimized in hundreds of different ways. By the time that they reach age 18, perhaps as high as 95 percent of our children have been victimized with child abuse in one form or another. It has to stop for the sake of our children, for the sake of our country — it has to stop. Let's ride the wave of this heightened awareness of child abuse to its completion. Any child's innocence is worth the effort, and every child has a right to protection, right across the board.

13
Nation's Constitutional Order in Crisis
We Hold These Truths

(July 4th, 1997 statement by prominent religious leaders)

"Government by the consent of the governed has been thrown into question, and as a result our constitutional order is in crisis," some 40 U.S. religious leaders declared in a July 4 statement. "Disordered liberty" represents "the great threat to the American experiment today. That disorder is increasingly expressed in a denial of the very concept of moral truth." All are responsible for the state of the nation, the statement added, but it said that on this occasion "our attention must be directed to the role of the courts in the disordering of our liberty.... In recent years, power has again and again been wielded, notably by the courts, without the consent of the governed." The statement said its concern "is by no means limited to the question of abortion, but the judicially imposed abortion license is at the very core of the disordering of our liberty." Furthermore, it said, "under the doctrine declared by the (Supreme Court), it would seem that individual choice can always take precedence over the common good." Pointing also to the role of elected leaders, the statement said that "today we are again in desperate need of political leaders who accept the responsibility to lead in restoring government derived from the consent of the governed."

Among the mainly Catholic, Evangelical and Orthodox signers of this statement issued in 1997 were Cardinals John O'Connor of New York, Anthony Bevilacqua of Philadelphia and Adam Maida of Detroit and 10 other Catholic bishops. A list of the signers appears at the conclusion of the statement. The statement follows:

"On this 221st anniversary of the Declaration of Independence, we join in giving thanks to almighty God for what the founders called this American experiment in ordered liberty. In the year of our Lord, 1997, the experiment is deeply troubled but it has not failed and, pease God, will not fail. As America has been a blessing to our forebears and to us, so will it be a blessing to future generations if we keep faith with the founding vision.

The Law of Nature and the Law of Nature's God

Invoking 'the law of nature and of nature's God,' the founders declared 'we hold these truths to be self-evident.' This Fourth of July, Americans must ask themselves whether they hold them still. We, for our part, answer emphatically in the affirmative. We affirm that before God and the law all are equal, 'endowed by their Creator with certain inalienable rights, that among these are life, liberty, and the pursuit of happiness.' In recent years, it has become increasingly manifest that these truths cannot be taken for granted. Indeed, there is ominous evidence of their rejection in our public life and law.

Religion and Morality are Indispensable

As leaders of diverse churches and Christian communities, we address our fellow citizens with no partisan political purpose. Our purpose is to help repair a contract too often broken and a covenant too often betrayed. We recall and embrace the wisdom of our first president, who declared in his farewell address: 'Of all the dispositions and habits which lead to political prosperity, religion and morality are indispensable supports. In vain would that man claim the tribute of patriotism, who should labor to subvert these great pillars of human happiness, these firmest props of the duties of men and citizens.' Religion and morality are not an alien intrusion upon our public life but the source and foundation of our pursuit of the common good.

It is in the nature of experiments that they can succeed, and they can fail. President Washington said in his first inaugural address: 'The preservation of the sacred fire of liberty and the destiny of the republican model of government are justly considered as deeply, perhaps as finally staked, on the experiment entrusted to the hands of the American people.' We urge the Christians of America to join us in a candid acknowledgment that we have not been as faithful as we ought to that great trust.

Nations Judged

Nations are ultimately judged not by their military might or economic wealth but by their fidelity to 'the laws of nature and of nature's God.' In the view of the founders, just government is self-government. Liberty is not license but is 'ordered liberty' — liberty in response to moral truth. The great threat to the American experiment today is not from enemies abroad but from disordered liberty. That disorder is increasingly expressed in a denial of the very concept of moral truth. The cynical question of Pontius Pilate, 'What is truth?' is today frequently taken to be a mark of sophistication also in our political discourse and even in the jurisprudence of our courts.

The bitter consequences of disordered liberty resulting from the denial of moral truth are by now painfully familiar. Abortion, crime, consumerism, drug abuse, family disintegration, teen-age suicide, neglect of the poor, pornography, racial prejudice, ethnic separatism and suspicion — all are rampant in our society. In politics, the public interest is too often sacrificed to private advantage; in economic and foreign policy, the lust for profits overrides concern for the well-being of families at home and the protection of human rights abroad. The powerful forget their obligation to the powerless, and the politics of the common good is abandoned in the interminable contention of special interests. We cannot boast of what we have made of the experiment entrusted to our hands.

While we are all responsible for the state of the nation and while our ills no doubt have many causes, on this Fourth of July our attention must be directed to the role of the courts in the disordering of our liberty. Our nation was constituted by the agreement that 'we the people,' through the representative institutions of republican government, would deliberate and decide how we ought to order our life together. In recent years that agreement has been broken. The declaration declares that 'governments are instituted among men, deriving their just powers from the consent of the governed.' In recent years, power has again and again been wielded, notably by the courts, without the consent of the governed.

Abortion on Demand

The most egregious instance of such usurpation of power is the 1973 decision of the Supreme Court in which it claimed to have discovered a 'privacy' right to abortion and by which it abolished, in what many constitutional scholars have called an act of raw judicial power, the abortion law of all 50 states. Traditionally in our jurisprudence, the law reflected the moral traditions by which people govern their lives. This decision was a radical departure, arbitrarily uprooting those moral traditions as they had been enacted in law through our representative political process. Our concern is for both the integrity of our constitutional order and for the unborn, whom the court has unjustly excluded from the protection of law.

Disordered Liberty

Our concern is by no means limited to the question of abortion, but the judicially imposed abortion license is at the very core of the disordering of our liberty. The question of abortion is the question of who belongs to the community for which we accept common responsibility. Our goal is unequivocal: every unborn child protected in law and welcomed in life. We have no illusions that, in a world wounded by sin, that goal will ever be achieved perfectly. Nor do we assume that at present all Americans agree with that goal. Plainly, many do not. We believe, however, that democratic deliberation and decision would result in laws much more protective of the unborn and other vulnerable human lives. We are convinced that the court was wrong, both morally and legally, to withdraw from a large part of the human community the constitutional guarantee of equal protection and due process of law.

Most Disagree

The American people as a whole have not accepted, and we believe they will not accept, the abortion regime imposed by Roe vs. Wade. In its procedural violation of democratic self-government and in its substantive violation of the 'laws of nature and of nature's God,' this decision of the court forfeits any claim to the obedience of conscientious citizens. We are resolved to work relentlessly, through peaceful and constitutional means and for however long it takes, to effectively reverse the abortion license imposed by Roe vs. Wade. We ask all Americans to join us in that resolve.

Responsible Self Government

The effort of 'we the people' to exercise the right and responsibility of self-government has been made even more difficult by subsequent decisions of the court. In its stated effort to end the national debate over abortion, the Supreme Court in Planned Parenthood vs. Casey (1992) transferred the legal ground for the abortion license from the implied right of privacy to an explicit liberty right under the 14th Amendment. The court there proposed a sweeping redefinition of liberty: 'At the heart of liberty is the right to define one's own concept of existence, of meaning of the universe and of the mystery of human life.' The doctrine declared by the court would seem to mean that liberty is nothing more nor less than what is chosen by the autonomous, unencumbered self.

Antithesis of Law

This is the very antithesis of the ordered liberty affirmed by the founders. Liberty in this debased sense is utterly disengaged from the concepts of responsibility and community and is pitted against the 'laws of nature and of nature's God.' Such liberty degenerates into license for the oppression of the vulnerable while the government looks the other way and throws into question the very possibility of the rule of law itself. Casey raises the serious question as to whether any law can be enacted in pursuit of the common good, for virtually any law can offend some individuals' definition of selfhood, existence and the meaning of life. Under the doctrine declared by the court, it would seem that individual choice can always take precedence over the common good.

14
Separation of Church and State
Not Separation of God from State

Our Founding Fathers

Our Founding Fathers set this great nation of ours upon the twin pillars of religion and morality. The First Amendment never intended to separate Christian principles from government. Yet today we so often hear the First Amendment coupled with the phrase "separation of church and state." The First Amendment simply states:

"Congress shall make no law respecting an establishment of religion or prohibiting the free exercise thereof."

Obviously, the words "separation," "church," or "state" are not found in the First Amendment; furthermore, that phrase appears in no founding document.

While most recognize the phrase "separation of church and

state," few know its source; but it is important to understand the origins of that phrase. What is the history of the First Amendment?

The process of drafting the First Amendment made the intent of the Founders abundantly clear; for before they approved the final wording, the First Amendment went through nearly a dozen different iterations and extensive discussions.

Those discussions—recorded in the Congressional Records from June 7 through September 25 of 1789—make clear their intent for the First Amendment. By it, the Founders were saying: "We do not want in America what we had in Great Britain: we don't want one denomination running the nation. We will not all be Catholics, or Anglicans, or any other single denomination. We do want God's principles, but we don't want one denomination running the nation."

This intent was well understood, as evidenced by court rulings after the First Amendment. For example, a 1799 court declared:

"By our form of government, the Christian religion is the established religion; and all sects and denominations of Christians are placed on the same equal footing."

Again, note the emphasis: "We do want Christian principles— we do want God's principles—but we don't want one denomination to run the nation."

In 1801, the Danbury Baptist Association of Danbury, Connecticut, heard a rumor that the Congregationalist denomination was about to be made the national denomination. That rumor distressed the Danbury Baptists, as it should have. Consequently, they fired off a letter to President Thomas Jefferson voicing their concern. On January 1, 1802, Jefferson wrote the Danbury Baptists, assuring them that "the First Amendment has erected a wall of separation between church and state."

His letter explained that they need not fear the establishment of a national denomination, and that, while the wall of the First Amendment would protect the church from government control, there would always be open and free expression of all orthodox religious practices and duties, for true religious expressions of faith would never threaten the purpose of government. Interference by government with a religious activity constituted a direct menace to the government and to the overall peace and good order of society. (Later, the Supreme Court identified potential "religious" activities in which the government might interfere: activities such as human sacrifice, bigamy, polygamy, the advocation of immorality or licentiousness, etc. If any of these activities were to occur in the name of "religion," then the government would interfere, for these were activities which threaten public peace and safety; but with orthodox religious practices, the government would not interfere).

Today, all that is heard of Jefferson's letter is the phrase, "a wall of separation between church and state," without either the context or the explanation given in the letter, or its application by earlier courts. The clear understanding of the First Amendment for a century-and-a-half was that it prohibited the establishment of a single national denomination. National policies and rulings in that century-and-a-half always reflected that interpretation.

For example, in 1853, a group petitioned Congress to separate Christian principles from government. They desired a so-called "separation of church and state" with chaplains being turned out of the Congress, the military, etc. Their petition was referred to the House and the Senate Judiciary Committees, which investigated for almost a year to see if it would be possible to separate Christian principles from government.

Both the House and the Senate Judiciary Committees returned with their reports. The following are excerpts from the House report delivered on Mary 27, 1854 (the Senate report was very similar):

"Had the people [the Founding Fathers], during the Revolution, had a suspicion of any attempt to war against Christianity, that Revolution would have been strangled in its cradle. At the time of the adoption of the Constitution and the amendments, the universal sentiment was that Christianity should be encouraged, but not any one sect [denomination]. . . . In this age, there is no substitute for Christianity. . . . That was the religion of the founders of the republic, and they expected it to remain the religion of their descendants."

Two months later, the Judiciary Committee made this strong

declaration:

"The great, vital, and conservative element in our system [the thing that holds our system together] is the belief of our people in the pure doctrines and divine truths of the Gospel of Jesus Christ."

The Committees explained that they would not separate these principles, for it was these principles and activities which had made us so successful—they had been our foundation, our basis.

During the 1870s, 1880s, and 1890s, yet another group which challenged specific Christian principles in government arrived before the Supreme Court. Jefferson's letter had remained unused for years, for as time had progressed after its use in 1802—and after no national denomination had been established—his letter had fallen into obscurity. But now—75 years later—in the case Reynolds *v.* United States, the plaintiffs resurrected Jefferson's letter, hoping to use it to their advantage.

In that case, the Court printed a lengthy segment of Jefferson's letter and then used his letter on "separation of church and state" to again prove that it was permissible to maintain Christian values, principles, and practices in official policy. For the next 15 years during that legal controversy, the Supreme Court utilized Jefferson's letter to ensure that Christian principles remained a part of government.

Following this controversy, Jefferson's letter again fell into disuse. It then remained silent for the next 70 years until 1947, when, in Everson *v.* Board of Education, the Court, for the first time, did not cite Jefferson's entire letter, but selected only eight words from it. The Court now announced:

"The First Amendment has erected 'a wall of separation between church and state.' That wall must be kept high and impregnable."

This was a new philosophy for the Court. Why would the Court take Jefferson's letter completely out of context and cite only eight of its words? Dr. William James, the father of modern psychology—and a strong opponent of religious principles in government and education—perhaps explained the Court's new strategy when he stated:

"There is nothing so absurd but if you repeat it often enough people will believe it."

This statement precisely describes the tact utilized by the Court in the years following its 1947 announcement. The Court began regularly to speak of a "separation of church and state," broadly explaining that, "This is what the Founders wanted—separation of church and state. This was their great intent." The Court failed to quote the Founders; it just generically asserted that this is what the Founders wanted.

The Courts continued on this track so steadily that, in 1958, in a case called Baer *v.* Kolmorgen, one of the judges was tired of hearing the phrase and wrote a dissent warning that if the court did not stop talking about the "separation of church and state," people were going to start thinking it was part of the Constitution. That warning was in 1958!

Nevertheless, the Court continued to talk about separation until June 25th, 1962, when, in the case Engle *v.* Vitale, the Court delivered the first ever ruling which completely separated Christian principles from education.

Secular Humanism

With that case, a whole new trend was established and secular humanism became the religion of America. In 1992 the Supreme Court stated the unthinkable: "At the heart of liberty is the right to define one's own concept of existence, of meaning, of the universe, and of the mystery of human life."

In 1997, as quoted earlier in these pages, 40 prominent Catholic and Protestant scholars wrote a position paper entitled *"We Hold These Truths"* in which they stated, "This is the very antithesis of the ordered liberty affirmed by the Founders. Liberty in this debased sense is utterly disengaged from the concept of responsibility and community and is pitted against the 'laws of nature and the laws of nature's God.' Such liberty degenerates into license and throws into question the very possibility of the rule of law itself."

Transcript of the Danbury Baptist
Letter to Thomas Jefferson
(For an exemplary analysis of the context of this exchange between the Danbury Baptists and Jefferson, see Daniel L Dreisbach's "Sowing Useful Truths and Principles": The Danbury Baptists, Thomas Jefferson, and the 'Wall of Separation'" in the *Journal of Church and State*, Vol. 39, Summer 1997.)

The address of the Danbury Baptist Association in the State of Connecticut, assembled October 7, 1801.

To Thomas Jefferson, Esq., President of the United States of America.

An Opening Greeting
Sir,

Among the many millions in America and Europe who rejoice in your election to office, we embrace the first opportunity which we have enjoyed in our collective capacity, since your inauguration, to express our great satisfaction in your appointment to the Chief Magistrate in the United States. And though the mode of expression may be less courtly and pompous than what many others clothe their addresses with, we beg you, sir, to believe, that none is more sincere.

Religious Freedom
Our sentiments are uniformly on the side of religious liberty: that Religion is at all times and places a matter between God and individuals, that no man ought to suffer in name, person, or effects on account of his religious opinions, [and] that the legitimate power of civil government extends no further than to punish the man who works ill to his neighbor. But sir, our constitution of government is not specific. Our ancient charter, together with the laws made coincident therewith, were adapted as the basis of our government at the time of our revolution.

Religion - First Object of Law

And such has been our laws and usages, and such still are, [so] that Religion is considered as the first object of Legislation, and therefore what religious privileges we enjoy (as a minor part of the State) we enjoy as favors granted, and not as inalienable rights, and these favors we receive at the expense of such degrading acknowledgments, as are inconsistent with the rights of freemen. It is not to be wondered at therefore, if those who seek after power and gain, under the pretense of government and Religion, should reproach their fellow men, [or] should reproach their Chief Magistrate, as an enemy of religion, law, and good order, because he will not, dares not, assume the prerogative of Jehovah and make laws to govern the Kingdom of Christ.

Sir, we are sensible that the President of the United States is not the National Legislator and also sensible that the national government cannot destroy the laws of each State, but our hopes are strong that the sentiment of our beloved President, which have had such genial effect already, like the radiant beams of the sun, will shine and prevail through all these States—and all the world—until hierarchy and tyranny be destroyed from the earth. Sir, when we reflect on your past services, and see a glow of philanthropy and goodwill shining forth in a course of more than thirty years, we have reason to believe that America's God has raised you up to fill the Chair of State out of that goodwill which he bears to the millions which you preside over.

May God Strengthen You for Your God-Appointed Task

May God strengthen you for the arduous task which providence and the voice of the people have called you—to sustain and support you and your Administration against all the predetermined opposition of those who wish to rise to wealth and importance on the poverty and subjection of the people.

May the Lord Preserve You from Every Evil

And may the Lord preserve you safe from every evil and bring you at last to his Heavenly Kingdom through Jesus Christ our Glorious Mediator.

Signed in behalf of the Association,
Nehemiah Dodge }
Ephram Robbins } The Committee
Stephen S. Nelson } .

Separation of State from God - Not God from State

Jefferson's Reply
Messrs. Nehemiah Dodge, Ephraim Robbins, and Stephen S.
Nelson
A Committee of the Danbury Baptist Association, in the State of
Connecticut.
Washington, January 1, 1802

Sentiments of Esteem
Gentlemen,—The affectionate sentiment of esteem and approbation which you are so good as to express towards me, on behalf
of the Danbury Baptist Association, give me the highest satisfaction. My duties dictate a faithful and zealous pursuit of the interests of my constituents, and in proportion as they are persuaded of
my fidelity to those duties, the discharge of them becomes more
and more pleasing.

Religion Is Between the Person and Their God
Believing with you that religion is a matter which lies solely
between man and his God, that he owes account to none other for
his faith or his worship, that the legislative powers of government
reach actions only, and not opinions, I contemplate with sovereign
reverence that act of the whole American people which declared
that their legislature would "make no law respecting an establishment of religion, or prohibiting the free exercise thereof," thus building a wall of separation between Church and State. Adhering to
this expression of the supreme will of the nation in behalf of the
rights of conscience, I shall see with sincere satisfaction the progress
of those sentiments which tend to restore to man all his natural
rights, convinced he has no natural right in opposition to his social
duties.

Reciprocation of Prayers

I reciprocate your kind prayers for the protection and blessing of the common Father and Creator of man, and tender you for your-selves and your religious association, assurances of my high respect and esteem.

RESOURCE: for more information contact:
WallBuilders
PO Box 397, Aledo, TX 76008 817.441.6044

15
Twelve Principles that are Leading Our Country to Ruin

From 1776 to 1962, these 12 principles were accepted and followed in our country. From 1962 onward, America has been on a downward spiral, slouching towards Gomorrah. What are the 12 principles of that downward curve?

I. Secular Humanism

First, secular humanism. In 1933 and again in 1973, prominent men in America signed the Humanist Manifesto which stated that man, and not God, is in charge of all things. This manifesto went on to reject any belief in God or religion. John Dewey, one of the signers, is the founder of modern progressive, liberal education.

Tenets 1, 2 and 3 were:

"Religious humanists regard the universe as self existing and not created."

"Humanism believes that man is a part of nature and that he has emerged as the result of a continuous process (evolution)."

"Holding an organic view of life, humanists find that the traditional dualism of mind and body must be rejected." Charles Francis Potter, a manifesto signer stated, "Education is the most powerful ally of humanism, and every American school is a school of Humanism."

These new humanists rejected almost 200 years of American history and philosophy.

Tenets 4, 5, 6 Stated:

"Humanism recognizes that man's religious culture and civilization, as clearly depicted by anthropology and history, are the products of a gradual development due to his interaction with his natural environment and with his social heritage. The individual born into a particular culture is largely molded to that culture."

"Humanism asserts that the nature of the universe depicted by modern science makes unacceptable any supernatural or cosmic guarantees of human values."

"We are convinced that the time has passed for theism, deism, modernism, and the several varieties of 'new thought.'"

Tenets 7, 8, 9 and 10 Stated:

"Religion consists of those actions, purposes, and experiences which are humanly significant. Nothing human is alien to the religious. . ."

"Religious humanism considers the complete realization of human personality to be the end of man's life and seeks its development and fulfillment in the here and now. . ."

"In place of the old attitudes involved in worship and prayer, the humanist finds his religious emotions expressed in a heightened sense of personal life and in a cooperative effort to promote social well-being."

"It follows that there will be no uniquely religious emotions and attitudes of the kind hitherto associated with belief in the supernatural."

Tenets 11, 12, and 13 Stated:

"Man will learn to face the crises of life in terms of his knowledge of their naturalness and probability. Reasonable and manly attitudes will be fostered by education and supported by custom..."

"Believing that religion must work increasingly for joy in living, religious humanists aim to foster the creative in man and to encourage achievements that add to the satisfactions of life."

"Religious humanism maintains that all associations and institutions exist for the fulfillment of human life. The intelligent evaluation, transformation, control, and direction of such associations and institutions with a view to the enhancement of human life is the purpose and program of humanism. Certainly religious institutions. . .and communal activities must be reconstituted as rapidly as experience allows, in order to function effectively in the modern world."

Tenets 14 and 15 Stated:

"The humanists are firmly convinced that existing acquisitive and profit-motivated society has shown itself to be inadequate and that a radical change in methods, controls, and motives must be instituted. A social and cooperative economic order must be established to the end that the equitable distribution of the means of life be possible. The goal of humanism is a free and universal society in which people voluntarily and intelligently cooperate for the common good. Humanists demand a shared life in a shared world."

"We assert that humanism will: (a) affirm life rather than deny it; (b) seek to elicit the possibilities of life, not flee from it; and (c) endeavor to establish the conditions of a satisfactory life for all, not merely for a few. . ."

II. No Longer A Nation Under God

Two, the separation of state from God. Until 1962 we were a nation under God. But then, five members of our Supreme Court did something unconstitutional. They made a law prohibiting the free exercise of religion. It was a law that would have far reaching consequences for it prohibited the two most vulnerable groups - teachers and students — first of all from praying and second of all from following the Ten Commandments.

The downward spiral in education and society has caused the greatest cultural shift in American history. Every known social evil including promiscuity, pornography, sexually-transmitted disease, teenage pregnancy, drug use, low SAT scores, violence, vulgarity, and even murder have escalated frighteningly in American schools. In many large cities, we use the expression - an educational meltdown. Last year, 70,000 high school students could not read their own diplomas.

III. Right To Life No Longer God Given Nor Inalienable

Three, abortion on demand. Beginning in 1973 with Roe *v.* Wade, we no longer held that human life was endowed by our Creator with certain inalienable rights, the first of which is the right to life; and we began the wholesale slaughter of unborn American citizens. This has been the greatest scourge to our land.

IV. Marriage No Longer Considered God Ordained And Sacred

Four, divorce on demand. Since 1962, there has been an escalation in the breakdown of family life, especially through divorce. No longer do the courts frown on divorce. They, in fact, encourage it in every way possible. For many millions of American young people, marriage, itself, is expendable. 65 percent of all marriages of people under 30 end in divorce within the first five years of marriage.

V. Common Decency Rejected

Five, pornography on demand. People falsely claiming First Amendment rights have made pornography to be part of mainstream America. It proliferates our screens — TV and the Internet — our magazines and unfortunately, our minds and our hearts. Throughout the world, the image of America is that we are a nation of low morals, for we have exported our pornography abroad.

VI. Wide Spread Violation Of The Natural Law

Six, the homosexual revolution. Disassociating morality from law, we are encountering a homosexual revolution. Everywhere you turn, you hear "Gay Rights." Many peolpe do not want to exclude active sodomists from the military or leadership in such organizations as the Boy Scouts. Millions of American youth are being deceived through the efforts of Planned Parenthood, the

People of the American Way, and Gay Rights groups and lobby-ists. Very young children are being taught to accept homosexual couples as the norm. And now, there is a move to authenticate homosexual "marriages".

VII. Sacredness of Sex Denied

Seven, the sexual revolution. Beginning in the sixties with the advent of modern American permissiveness, promoted first by rock and roll and then by heavy rock music, we have seen a shocking explosion in promiscuity especially among young people. Tradi-tional Christian modesty and virtue is mocked, even in college class-rooms. And co-ed dorms have become the norm on college cam-puses. Promiscuity now has become mainstream America. And most young people are now psychologically and sociologically unfit to enter a traditional Judaic-Christian marriage.

VIII. Traditional Dignity of Women Rejected

Eight, the women's movement. Hand-in-hand with the sexual revolution is the modern American liberation movement in which women have attempted to free themselves of any restraint that might have come from moral or religious conviction. Many millions of women claim freedom of their own bodies, not only to prostitute them but also to abort any children that might result from promis-cuous activity. Traditional feminine virtue and mission have been severely threatened by the onslaught of the feminist and the sexual revolution.

IX. The Media Becomes A Medium Of Evil

Nine, the media. The media in America bears much of the blame for the collapse of traditional American values. It has not been, by and large, pro-God, pro-family or pro-life. It has attacked the Christian church on almost every front, especially in the areas of religion and morality.

X. The Legal Profession Now Legalizes Evil

Ten, the legal profession. The legal profession has so prosti-tuted itself that lawyers have made what was traditionally right to seem wrong, and what was traditionally wrong to seem right. They've turned each commandment upside down. The first commandment they violate by talking about separation of Church and state. The second commandment is violated by allowing profanity to go unchecked in favor of free speech. The third commandment is violated because they object to what used to be called "Blue Laws." The fourth commandment is violated by seeking abortions without parental consent and by too-freely entering into divorce cases. The fifth commandment is violated by our so-called pro-choice laws. The sixth commandment is virtually obliterated as sodomy, promiscuity and pornography are all protected by liberal laws. The eighth commandment is violated when lying is officially sanctioned, even when it occurs in the White House and our elected officials officially lie to cover up a lying president. It's hard to discover any area of evil that they do not endorse.

XI. The Medical Community Prostitutes Its Role

Eleven, the medical community. The medical community has forsaken its traditional role. The absolute scandal of the American medical community is that they are on record for being involved in the destruction of 100 million innocent unborn babies. They are also on record for being in support of stem cell research that would destroy human life.

XII. The Supreme Court Legislates A
Contradictory World View

Twelve, the Supreme Court. Of all the agencies in America that have betrayed the American ideal, the most flagrant is our Supreme Court itself. By a use of raw judicial power, they have set this nation on its great decline. They no longer uphold the laws of nature or the laws of nature's God or the God-given inalienable right to life of every American citizen. They have contradicted the Constitution over and again. In fact, they have set aside its basic principles by calling it, in liberal terms, "a living document." By that they mean they can contradict its basic tenets.

The legitimate purpose of government since the founding of America has been to protect the lives, liberty and prosperity of its citizens. James Madison summed it up well when he stated, "We have staked the whole future of American civilization not upon the power of government, far from it. We have staked the future of all our political institution upon the capacity of each and all of us to govern ourselves, to control ourselves, to sustain ourselves according to the Ten Commandments of God."

Our Founding Fathers based our system of government on the First Commandment, "Thou shalt have no other god before Me." They understood clearly that we were created to serve God, not the state. Since we were created in God's image, government according to their original vision should be an aid to secure man's God-endowed rights. They instituted a system of representative government with clear limits on what government could and could not do. This was clearly and meticulously carried out to ensure individual freedom.

Today our government is threatening our basic freedoms. U.S. Senator Jesse Helms provides the answer, "When you have men who no longer believe that God is in charge of human affairs, you have men attempting to take the place of God by means of the super state. The divine providence on which our forefathers relied has been supplanted by the providence of the All-Powerful State. I believe that this is the source of deep weakness in America, because it is a transgression of the first and greatest commandments."

Woodrow Wilson said, "The history of liberty is a history of limitation of governmental power, not the increase of it. When we resist, therefore, the concentration of power, we are resisting the powers of death, because concentration of power is what always precedes the destruction of human liberties."

16
12 Widely Held Myths Resulting From Our Decline

I. The Battle Isn't Real

Recently somebody asked a young person, "Do you know what the two greatest problems in America are?" "I don't know and I don't care." the youth responded. "Wow, you got both of them."

the older person replied. Although our nation is reveling in accesses, rolling in luxuries, rollicking in pleasure, revolting in morals and rotting in sin, most young people and many older ones, as well, do not know it and they don't care. Not until all is lost will many awake to the painful reality that the United States of America, as it was, is now gone. As a humanistic society moves further and further away from Judaic-Christian values, it will become increasingly tolerant of competing viewpoints.

Traditional Americans are now considered part of the radical religious right. Clearly, two world views are on a collision course. Millions of people have been killed in the twentieth century alone. Thirty million have been Chinese, 60 million have been Russian and 15 million died under Hitler. Communism, Fascism, and Nazism have this in common—all were godless and humanistic and all rejected the sanctity of human life.

II. Life Began With Blind Chance

Many people today believe in the "Big Bang" theory, as foolish as it is. Although the doctrine of evolution is in a scientific state of disarray, the average American does not realize it. The head of the French Academy of Science candidly admitted, "Evolution is a fairy tale for adults." This is not what the public at large is hearing, nor what American school children are being taught. Clarence Darrow once argued in the 1925 Scopes Trial that it is "Bigotry for public schools to teach only one theory of origin."

Since evolution is entrenched in public education, the American Civil Liberties Union insists that only one theory of origin be taught. Bigotry has returned in full force. To settle for evolution or the "Big Bang" theory without God begs a thousand scientific questions. Author Aldous Huxley once responded to a question as to why evolution was readily accepted. He admitted, "The reason we accepted Darwinism, even without proof, is because we didn't want God to interfere with our sexual mores." While many scientists admit the evidence for the evolutionary fairy tale is crumbling, they refuse to run towards God. If man is only a biological accident, (the product of chance chemical reactions of impersonal forces), it is virtually impossible for him to decide right from wrong.

Without God, we cannot have a moral law.

III. We Can Have Morality Without Religion

In 1980 the Supreme Court struck down a Kentucky law that required the posting of The Ten Commandments in public school classrooms. The court said that The Ten Commandments were "plainly religious. . .and may induce children to read, meditate upon, perhaps to venerate and to obey the commandments."

Morality and religion can never be separated. The very basis of morality is a wise, holy and loving God. Ironically, humanists at times talk about morality — the morality that they borrow from the Judaic-Christian ethic. When they say that they do not believe in killing in general, rape in general, breaking and entering, violence to children, the sexual harassment of women, they are assuming a world view that contains the Ten Commandments. We have not yet fully seen the results of this humanistic decline because a large part of America is still coasting on the values derived from our rich Judeo-Christian heritage. What about the upcoming generations? As our heritage fades, young people will be permitted to do whatever seems right in the wrong eyes of a world with twisted values where bad becomes good and good becomes bad.

IV. Whatever Is Legal Is Moral

At the war crimes trial in Nuremberg, Germany, Hitler's henchmen argued that they had broken no laws. Germany's own legal system, they contended, permitted the elimination of those who impeded the advance of the Third Reich. Adolph Eichmann protested before his execution, "I had to obey the laws of war and my flag." In our own country, a group protesting an abortion clinic were charged with slander because they had called abortionists "murderers." The abortionists argued, as had the accused at Nuremberg: You can't call someone who isn't breaking a law a murderer.

Both the experience of Nuremberg and today's silent holocaust in our abortion clinics bear eloquent witness to the fact that when a state believes it is accountable to no one except itself, it assumes a hidden premise: that whatever is legal is moral. Robert H. Jackson, chief counsel for the United States in the Nuremberg trials, was forced to appeal to permanent values, to moral standards transcending the lifestyles of a particular society. In effect, he argued that there is "a law beyond the law" that stood in judgment on the arbitrary changing opinions of men. Today the shape of America is being altered by use of the same strategy. The Supreme Court, influenced by the humanistic trends, has helped to brainwash our people to believe that whatever is legal is moral. They would argue that there is no law above human laws.

This is not the case of our Founding Fathers. Whether individually Christian or not, there was a general consensus of theism, the belief that God existed and the new republic was based upon this fundamental truth. This understanding profoundly influenced their view of law and government. As the Christian world view has faded, America has turned not to the laws of God, but to what Francis Schaeffer called "sociological law": that is. . .Law is only what the majority wants, or what the judge says it is. Thus, in 1973 the Supreme Court invalidated the abortion laws of fifty states and legalized abortion on demand. Where did the Court get the notion that a woman has a right to an abortion? Such right is not found in the Constitution. The Court made it up. Like Napoleon, it crowned itself emperor—answerable to no one—not even to the American people. Such distortion of "rights" has also opened the doors to pornography (under the guise of a free press) and to the offense of the public at large. As Christians, we must explode the myth that whatever is legal is moral. What men make legal is not necessarily moral.

V. Morality Cannot Be Legislated

Secular humanists would like us to believe that they are broadminded, pluralistic and neutral in moral matters. They are opposed to censorship, sectarianism and intolerance. The media has done a successful job of getting the American people to believe that it is the so-called right wing religious fanatics who are seeking to "impose their morality on society." But all laws are an imposition of someone's morality. That is why the statement, "You cannot legislate morality", as it stands, is absurd. Secular humanism is imposing its own morality on the American public. It does so through the media, the schools and the courts. There is a clear intent to keep Christian thinking out of the mainstream of the media and the nation's political life. When Francis Schaeffer's film, *Whatever Happened to the Human Race?* was shown on a television station in Washington, pro-abortionists exerted all the influence they could to prevent it from being aired. (Liberal establishments are strangely silent about the pluralism and open mindedness they verbally espouse when the cause contradicts their own.) Even after the showing, the *Washington Post* ran an article entitled, "No Matter How Moving, Show Still Propaganda." Thus the media ridiculed the program with loaded terminology.

Only The Scandals

One editor admitted that the only religious news story that the press likes to do is a scandal. When a book entitled, "How to Have Sex With Children," was confiscated by the Chicago police, several demonstrators marched in protest, insisting that pornographers should have unlimited privileges. But neither prayer nor a creationist view is allowed in the classroom. As columnist George Will put it so ably, "And it is, by now, a scandal beyond irony that, thanks to the energetic litigation of 'civil liberties' fanatics, pornographers enjoy expansive first amendment protection while first graders in a nativity play are said to violate first amendment values."

No Law Neutral

No law is neutral. Every law imposes some form of morality on society. Abortionists impose their morality on the unborn. Homosexuals want their views flaunted in the public school classrooms. Atheists want religious influence excluded from public life. Some politicians, in an attempt to remain "neutral" on such issues as abortion in order to sidestep the flak, say they are personally opposed to abortion but "would never impose their values on society." If so, how does this sound? "I personally would never gas a Jew, but I have no right to impose my moral judgment on the Nazis. . . I don't think the courts have the right to reach into someone's private gas chamber and legislate morality." Forty percent of college history majors in the United States will not admit that the Holocaust was immoral according to John DeLeo in an article entitled "Absolute Phobia" in a recent edition of *U.S. News & World Report*.

The Real Question

The question is not whether the public will allow religion to "impose its morality" on America. Morality will be imposed. The real question is: Whose morality will be legislated?

VI. The Role Of Men And Women Is Inter-Changeable

On the surface, it may seem that every Christian should be in favor of such legislation as the ERA. If we take seriously the biblical teaching that women are created in the image of God, they certainly are entitled to equal rights. Yet behind the proposed amendment lies a deception. If the ERA had been ratified, it would have brought a sweeping restructure of society, with a devastating attack on the family and morality in general. The amendment would likely destroy America, as we know it.

The radical feminists who so vociferously back the movement want, first of all, to end the institution of marriage. Sheila Cronan speaks for many of them when she writes, "Since marriage constitutes slavery for women, it is clear that the Women's Movement must concentrate on attacking this institution. Freedom for women cannot be won without the abolition of marriage."

These same feminists want freedom from the burden of children. There can be no equality, they insist, as long as the woman is a homemaker. Moreover, the children, they say, should be reared by another, namely the state. The Houston Conference for Women, sponsored by N.O.W., called for federally-funded day care centers around the clock, seven days a week. Society as a whole, they insist, should bear the burden. Lenin pursued this philosophy in Russia. So has Cuba and Communist China. It is a Marxist solution.

The National Organization for Women opposed the right of churches to make any differentiation between men and women.

The refusal to ordain homosexuals could soon be interpreted as "contrary to public policy," and homosexual teachers could flaunt their lifestyle in the public classroom. Meanwhile, in an incredibly ridiculous project, the World Council of Churches has released a Biblical Lectionary that omits all gender based terms, including all reference to God as "He." Both the Scriptures, and the overwhelming majority of the public at large, still make clear distinctions between male and female. To disregard these differences is to invite the disintegration of America.

VII. A Fetus Is Not Human

This very day, as you read this article, some 4,300 preborn babies will legally be put to death—under the protection of the Supreme Court's 1973 decision in Roe *vs*. Wade. In earlier days, abortion was the last act of a desperate woman. Today it is said that 97% of all abortions occur simply for convenience. It has become the nation's method of choice for birth control. Wrote Peter Singer in *Pediatrics*, "We can no longer base our ethics on the idea that human beings are a special form of creation made in the image of God and singled out from all other animals." Babies' bodies have been sold by the bag. They are used in some cosmetics and for experimentation. In one general hospital, the sale of aborted babies brought in $68,000 in a ten-year period.

Justice Harry Blackman, author of the 64-page document that came from the Roe *vs*. Wade decision, said that objection to abortion came mainly from two sources: the oath of Hippocrates and Christianity. Since the oath specifically forbids abortion, the Court wrestled with its influence but concluded that, in the context of general opinion, "ancient religions did not bar abortion." As for Christianity, it was apparently dismissed by the court because of the separation of Church and state. In effect, the Court omitted two thousand years of Judeo-Christian influence and reached back into paganism to find a basis for its moral judgment. Those who have studied the document in detail confess that it is a mix of illogical reasoning and nonsequiturs.

Justice Byron White dissented on the decision and said, "I find nothing in the language or history of the Constitution to support the Court's judgment." As a result of the tragic decision, more than 40 million unborn children have had their lives snuffed out— more than twenty times the total number of Americans lost in all of our nation's wars. Today, abortion is big business. With 1.5 million each year, at an average cost of $350 each, abortion clinics are raking in thousands of dollars daily. How could our justices have blundered so badly? The answer: they bowed to the pressure of feminists who were calling for abortion on demand as a legitimate right. It is what happened on the bench one hundred years ago when the Dred Scott decision denied the black his right to freedom and relegated blacks to the status of "nonpersons" . . . for personal convenience. The decision was also the result of the "new morality" of the sixties. Seventy-five percent of all those who have abortions are unmarried. Abortion has become the "mopping up operation" from a breakdown in moral values.

VIII. We Can Ignore The Ghost Of Karl Marx

We can ignore the ghost of Karl Marx, Adolph Hitler, Joseph Stalin and Benito Mussolini. In the 20th century, America watched the rise of three atheistic systems that did not appreciate the sanctity of human life. Because of Karl Marx, Joseph Stalin and Joseph Lenin, one hundred million people were murdered by Communism, which did not hold the inherent, inalienable, God-given right to life of the person. Marx's notion was that individuals have no inherent rights, only those conferred by the state. And those who stand in the way of the state's goals were completely eliminated. Clearly, the ghost of Marx was present when the Supreme Court gave our women an absolute right to kill their own child, without any interference by the father or grandparents of the child.

The Roe *v.* Wade decision stated, "The state has no compelling interest in the life of the unborn." As Woodrow Wilson said, "those who fail to study history are doomed to repeat it. Those who forget the past are doomed to relive it." Hitler founded an atheistic system called Nazism and he, too, had no view of the sanctity of human life. The only right a person had was those conferred by the Third Reich. And during the Second World War, which he started, 6 million innocent Jewish people were killed, 3 million Catholics, thousands of priests and nuns, and millions of others considered a threat to the regime, totaling 45 million people. Still today, there are many Americans who want to separate God from state and who do not respect the sanctity of human life. The ghost of Hitler still lingers over us because 12 million Jewish babies have been killed in the holocaust taking place here in the United States. Mussolini introduced Fascism into the Catholic country of Italy, which again was an atheistic system that did not acknowledge the sanctity of human life. As a consequence, countless millions of Italians were brought into the war while countless millions more were killed.

Nevertheless, radical feminism in this country has derived much of it vision from socialism. As Lenin put it, "We cannot be free if one half the population is enslaved in the kitchen." Nor can a country be free if parents have the right to teach their children religion. All the above "isms" place a firm wall between God and country. And all three failed to recognize the God-given, inalienable dignity of the life of the human person. Although the United States won the Second World War, the ghost of these tyrants still hangs over us.

IX - Pornography is a harmless adult pleasure.

Today, pornography is mainstream America. Our movies, magazines, songs and media are drowning in a sea of filth. Much of America is rotting on the inside. One half of all divorces take place because of adultery, often encouraged by pornography. In Michigan, 43 percent of over 35,000 sex crimes were pornography-related. No one can calculate the number of divorces, emotional scars, the bondage and the guilt that pornography has brought to our land. Yet for the past 8 years, pornography has gone on almost virtually unchecked. It is even more invasive now with the video, TV and Internet explosion.

X - the Church should have no voice in Government.

Beginning with the Humanist Manifesto of 1933, we have created a culture of secular humanism. As stated above, Humanists believe that neither God nor Church should have any voice in government. And yet, as Whitaker Chambers noted, "Humanism is not new. It is, in fact, man's second oldest faith. Its promise was whispered in the first days of creation under the tree of the knowledge of Good and Evil: 'You shall be as gods'."

XI - Truth is being broad-minded

The truth of the matter is that all truth is narrow, especially religious and moral truths. One plus one equals two, not three, or four, or even one-and-a-half, or two-and-one-quarter. No, one plus one equals only two. There are 50 states in these United States, Not 48 or 51, just 50 states and only 50 states. Not one more, nor one less. There are nine planets. Not eight, nor ten, just nine. Only a validly licensed and authorized pilot is allowed to pilot a 747 airplane and only a validly authorized doctor can perform surgery. In every single field, truth is narrow and not broad; but most especially in the area of ultimate truths—that is, religious truths. There is only one God. Jesus is His only and Incarnate Son. There are only Ten Commandments, not nine, nor eleven, and they are not suggestions, nor multiple choice, nor some man's subjective reasoning. There is only one Church, founded by Jesus as His Mystical Body. There are 27 Books in the New Testament and 45 in the Old Testament. There are seven Sacraments and twelve articles in the Apostle's Creed. And there have been 21 Ecumenical Councils that have used the infallible prophetic authority first given to Simon Peter in Caeseria Phillipi. Yes, all truth is narrow.

XII - A person has a right to sin.

In a highly permissive society, many begin to think that a person has a right to sin. But the truth is just the opposite. No one has a right to rob my house, to sodomize my spouse, to rape my daughter, or even to use offensive speech in my presence.

XIII - Freedom of Speech

Freedom of Speech should actually be freedom of responsible speech. Nobody has the right on a crowded airplane to stand up and cry out, "I am a terrorist and I have a bomb!" even if they may be joking. Nobody has a right to address a female secretary in explicitly sexual overtones. Nobody has a right to use obscene words in front of anyone but especially not in front of children.

The truth of the matter is that "freedom of speech" is a myth but freedom of responsible speech is not. All speech must be both free and responsible.

17
The New Tolerance

A new best-selling book by Josh McDowell and Bob Hostetler is entitled, *The New Tolerance* - with the subtitle "How a Cultural Movement Threatens to Destroy You, Your Faith, and Your Children." By unmasking the true nature of the cultural movement of "Tolerance," this paperback will not only help you to understand it, but equip you to counter its insidious effects on your faith, your family, your church, and your children. In addition, the authors teach you how to encounter and neutralize this threat by helping you to discern truth from error. Like it or not, we live in a post-Christian culture. What used to be a nation under God is now a nation separate from God, His Ten Commandents and His Spirit. The new culture of secular humanism has made man the measure of all things. It is also a culture of relativism that would trivialize and relativize the truth of the gospel.

"Truth and Tolerance"
Today's definition of tolerance goes beyond merely respecting a person's rights because the new tolerance declares that all beliefs are equally valid. Christians, or for that matter, anyone who believes in objective truth and morality will face increasing pressures to be silent about their convictions. Because to speak out at school, at work, or in the public forum will be seen as an intolerant judgment on sinful beliefs and evil lifestyles. Such pressure will pose severe problems not only for families but for children as well. This is illustrated by the case of Shannon Berry, a first grader at Bayshore elementary school in Bradenton, Florida. Shannon and a classmate were talking about Jesus one day during recess. A teacher pulled them aside and reprimanded them, telling them that they were not allowed to talk about Jesus at school. The rise of the new tolerance makes the sharing of faith an increasingly dangerous

proposition for many people who now believe not only in the separation of church from state but also in the separation of state from God.

"One Word Two Meanings"

The traditional definition of tolerance means simply to recognize and respect another persons valid beliefs and practices. The attitude based upon the dignity of the human person in the freedom of religious expression is what tolerance meant to most people. Today's definition is vastly different. The new tolerance considers every person's beliefs, values, and lifestyles no matter how sinful, pagan, or destructive as equally good and valid. Not only does everyone have equal rights to his beliefs, but all beliefs are considered equal. This new tolerance goes beyond respecting a person's rights. It demands praise and endorsement of every person's beliefs, values, and lifestyles no matter what they are. This fundamental shift in meaning represents one of the greatest shifts in history, certainly in the history of our country and most people are missing that.

"Dangerous Implications"

This new tolerance had many dangerous implications. Unless Christian churches and families recognize it, this new millennium is likely to be marked not only by much anti-Christian sentiment but also by the repression of public discourse. The issue is no longer the truth of the message but rather a belief that there is now absolute moral truth.

"No Ten Commandments"

In short, what is being stated today is that there is no Ten Commandments, no objective Judaic-Christian objective standard of morality. If you want to hold belief in God, or that murder, adultery, and sodomy are wrong, that's only your opinion. An opposite opinion would be held as equally valid and this is scary. The Ten Commandments are reduced to Ten Suggestions that Moses brought down from the mountain or they are some religious person's subjective and personal view of what is right or wrong.

"Politically Correct and Incorrect"

Actually, the situation is not quite that black and white. There is, at present, a politically correct gospel that most liberals agree with in union with conservatives but there's also a politically incorrect one. The politically correct gospel teaches that it is wrong to take drugs, to murder, to rob, to rape, to steal, to break and enter, to smoke in public places, to advertise cigarettes, and to sexually harass a person. When conservatives speak in these fields, they find that most liberals will agree with them. To this extent, both groups accept certain of the Ten Commandments, but there's a whole vast other field of Judaic-Christian values that would be called Politically Incorrect and therefore, must be tolerated. These would include sodomy, artificial contraception, divorce, co-habitation, pornography and abortion. When one dares to counter this field of "tolerance", one is immediately attacked or shot down. Here the Ten Commandments are definitely thrown out.

"Glaring Inconsistencies"

The inconsistencies of the new Tolerance are apparent. Even a liberal person is definitely not pro-choice when it comes to ordinary murder, breaking and entering, or rape. But they definitely are pro-Choice when it comes to the baby in the womb. Liberal people will not allow an alternative lifestyle for murderers, thieves, and rapists but they definitely do allow it for sodomists. People will be against the sexual harassment of a woman in the office yet will put that same woman in a pornographic film. The amount to which you can degrade, dehumanize and vulgarize her is literally limitless. Simply to point out to liberals that such glaring inconsistencies are not logical does not help. What is needed is a change of heart; what is called normally "conversion".

"Liberalism in the Court"

This new tolerance unfortunately has made its way even to the Supreme Court. In 1997, 40 United States religious leaders declared in a July 4th statement that the consent of the governed has been thrown into question. These religious leaders wrote "On this

221st anniversary of the Declaration of Independence, we join in giving thanks to almighty God for what the founders called this American experiment in ordered liberty. In the year of our Lord 1997, the experiment is deeply troubled but it has not failed and, please God, will not fail. As America has been a blessing to our forebears and to us, so will it be a blessing to future generations, if we keep faith with the founding vision."

"An Objective Order"

In the field of science, everyone admits that there are objective truths. There is a sun that shines by day and there is a moon that glows at night. So true is that, that we call the first day of the week Sunday and we call each period of 30 days a Month (Moon-th). There are 9 planets and we can name them. No one questions such truths and if one dared to question, they would be considered simply wrong. In the field of mathematics, it is the same. Two plus two equals 4 and not 5 or 3. This is not questioned, and if one should question it, they would simply be considered in error. Such truths are objective. They are out there for anyone to see. In the field of medicine, it is the same. We do not give any quack the license to operate on a patient in the hospital. Each doctor has to be certified by objective medical tests. It is not a question of private opinion; it is objective and true. No doctor is allowed to use dirty or unsanitary needles. It is simply wrong for everyone, no matter what their personal beliefs may be.

"All The More True"

This is all the more true in the field of theology. There is one God in three persons. This is not a matter of conjecture or opinion. It is true. And this true God gave to Moses Ten Commandments: that everyone must reverence God, respect His name, and keep holy His day. No one is allowed to be disobedient or murderous. Adultery, stealing, and lying are wrong for everyone everywhere and no one, under any circumstance, has the right to covet another person's spouse or goods. These are objective moral norms for everyone everywhere and for all times.

Conclusion

We must always remember, however, that when the apostle Peter told us, "Always be prepared to give an answer to everyone who asks you to give the reason for the hope that you have," he added, "but do this with gentleness and respect" (1 Pet 3:15).

We must aggressively practice love. Everyone loves love, it seems, but few recognize how incompatible love is with the new tolerance. The new tolerance simply avoids offending someone; but we must help our children live in love, which actively seeks to promote the good of another person.

The new tolerance says, "You must approve of what I do." Love responds, "I must do something harder; I will love you, even when your behavior offends me."

The new tolerance says, "You must agree with me." Love responds, "I must do something harder; I will tell you the truth because I am convinced 'the truth will set you free.'"

The new tolerance says, "You must allow me to have my way." Love responds, "I must do something harder; I will plead with you to follow the right way, because I believe you are worth the risk."

The new tolerance seeks to be inoffensive. Love takes risks.

The new tolerance glorifies division. Love seeks unity.

The new tolerance costs nothing. Love costs everything.

I believe the dreadful potential of the new tolerance can be averted, but only with a renewed commitment to truth, justice and love. And, as it happens, that powerful trio of virtues can do more than prevent disaster; it can bring about true community and culture in the midst of diversity and disagreement.

18

Of Everything Except Christ and the Church

In the March 18th issue of *US News and World Report*, the courageous John Leo wrote an article entitled *"With Bias Toward All"* stating clearly what most Americans take for granted: That the news media are damaging their own honesty and credibility by pushing a leftist anti-God, anti-Christian, anti-Catholic, anti-family, and anti-life agenda. Mr. Leo quotes from Bernard Goldberg's best-selling book, *Bias* that shows a disconnect between the way the media packages the news and the mindset of most Americans. Most Americans are still pro-God, pro-Church, pro-family, and pro-life. The media is not. For example, David Shaw, The *Los Angeles Times* media critic, in 1990 stunned everyone with the four-part series on the press coverage of the abortion issue. He essentially concluded that the American media is "so strongly pro-choice" that it cannot bring itself to report the issue fairly. And a former liberal darling of the media, Tammy Bruce, has a new book, *The New Thought Police: Inside the Left's Assault on Free Speech and Free Minds.*

Religious Bigotry and Holy Wars

Religious bigotry has been with us for centuries and many holy wars have been fought because of it. People of my generation have watched sadly as irreligious systems took over Russia, Italy, and Germany. We saw the rise of Communism, Fascism, and Nazism, all of which were irreligious. They suppressed religion and did not respect the sanctity of human life. As a result 100 million were murdered by Communists; 45 million were killed in World War II. If you go to Dachau or Auschwitz, they will show you that Jews and Catholics were killed side by side.

Catholic Church Greatest Friend
of the Jews During the Holocaust

The real story: Pope Pius XII was the greatest friend of the Jews during the holocaust! The real facts as the media hasn't presented them:

1. Pope Pius XII did more than any other person to save Jewish lives during the Holocaust, saving more that one million of them: 200,000 in Hungary, 50,000 in Poland, 360,000 in Bulgaria, 250,000 in Romania, 22,000 in Slovakia, and 120,000 in Italy.

2. At the risk of losing his neutrality and the risk of his own life, he ordered all Catholic convents, seminaries, monasteries, orphanages and hospitals to be open to hide our Jewish brothers and sisters.

117

3. In Rome occupied by Nazi troops, he harbored Jews within the Vatican itself to the extent that the Nazi's did in fact have a plan to invade and kill the Pope and others.

4. While secretary to Pope Pius XI, the future Pope Pius XII wrote an encyclical letter warning the German people of the dangers of Hitler and Nazism. This letter, written in German, was smuggled into Germany by Francis Spellman, the future Cardinal of New York.

5. Between 1936 and 1943, Pope Pius XII protested against Hitler and Nazism over 60 times. After the Dutch hierarchy officially protested the arrest and murder of Jews, Hitler retaliated so forcefully with the deaths of added Catholics and Jews that, along with the Red Cross, the Vatican realized that any future protests would bring down fierce measures of Nazi retaliation. From that point on all help for the Jews was carried out by the various underground organizations that were saving the Jews by the tens of thousands.

6. When the head rabbi of Rome had arranged significant funds as a ransom of Italian Jews, it was Pope Pius XII who raised most of the ransom. In fact, the head rabbi became a Catholic right after the war, taking the Pope's own name.

7. Righ after the war, the B'nai Brith Society named Pope Pius XII Man of the Year, and he was praised by every prominent Jewish leader from Golda Meir to the head rabbi of the United States.

8. When Adolf Eichmann's diaries were released by the Israeli government on March 1, 2000, Eichmann unwittingly exonerated Pope Pius XII for, as Eichmann wrote, Pope Pius XII "vigorously protested the arrest of Jews, calling for the interruption of such action, otherwise the Pope would denounce it publicly." Further on he stated in his diary, "At that time, my office received the copy of the letter (that I immediately gave to my direct superiors) sent by the Catholic Church in Rome, in the person of Bishop Hudal, to the commander of the German forces in Rome, General Stahel. The Church was vigorously protesting the arrest of Jews of Italian citizenship, requesting that such actions be interrupted throughout Rome and its surroundings. To the contrary, the Pope would denounce it publicly. The Curia was especially angry because these

incidents were taking place practically under Vatican windows. But, precisely at that time, without paying any attention to the Church's position, the Italian fascist government passed a law ordering the deportation of all Italian Jews to concentration camps."

"The objective given and the excessive delay in the steps necessary to complete the implementation of the operation, resulted in a great part of Italian Jews being able to hide and escape capture," Eichmann wrote. "A good number of them hid in convents or were helped by men and women of the Church."

Ireland

I saw what religious bigotry and hatred could do in the land of my forefathers I watched as anti-Catholic bigotry inflamed the hatred in many a protestant heart. I heard the rabid voice of Ian Paisley as he stood up for such bigotry and I watched the secular press inflame it as well, with equal horror. I watched Catholics respond with hatred, extreme violence, and murder. I have been to Northern Ireland and have seen the shrines and names of the martyrs killed by religious bigotry. I made it a point to visit John Hume, that holy man who was given the Nobel peace prize for bringing Catholics and Protestants together and getting them to sign a peace concordant that has held for years. The marvelous thing was that the Irish press fought for peace and against bigotry on both sides.

Israel

I have been to the Holy land and Jerusalem, the center of the world's great religion, and have witnessed what bigotry and hatred can do. And in all these cases, I have witnessed what a bigoted press and media can do on both sides, and I thanked God for America. This beautiful land that holds these truths to be self evident, that all men are created equal and can walk hand-in-hand, Protestants and Catholics, blacks and whites, Near East and Far East, men and women with yellow, black, brown, and white skins walking side by side under the yoke of American liberty.

An All Out Anti-Catholic Affront

Now this, our all too pagan and liberal press and media, have made an all out frontal attack on the Catholic Church. Never in modern history has the attack been so widespread. This issue is not, (I repeat is not) "child abuse." If it were, the press would be attacking child abuse in its many forms, most of which they allow, condone, or cover up.

The Catholic Church is Doing More than Any Other Institution in the United States to Address the Horror of Sexual Abuse of Minors. As Bishop Wilton Gregory, former president of the U.S. Conference of Catholic Bishops, originally stated, "I am very heartened by the professionals who work with both victims and abusers, who encourage us in this work because, they tell us, there is not another institution in the United States that is doing more to understand and address the horror of sexual abuse of minors."

An Unsurpassed Record

Any fair-minded person should realize the Catholic Church teaches a no-tolerance policy on abortion, pornography, artificial contraception, promiscuity, self-abuse, incest, homosexual acts, sodomy, and even deliberately consented to impure thoughts. On the positive side, the Church promotes the Gospel of Life, The Legion of Decency, and a Catholic school system that promotes virginity and purity. The Catholic Church holds up for everyone (along with certain Saints, such as Saint Cecilia and Saint Maria Goretti, who died to maintain their virginity), Mary, the Mother of God, as our model of purity . She has advocated prayer, frequent confession, modesty in dress, and the practice of mortification and penance. In all of history, no institution has done more to promote purity, as any fair-minded person will readily admit.

The media has a long history of viciously attacking Christ and His Church. The media pushes abortion (100 million of them so far). Christ and His Church teaches the sanctity of every human life, especially the unborn. The media advocates pornography as a First Amendment right. The Church does not. The Church advocates respect and dignity for all persons. The media publishes articles that dehumanize children. Christ objects to each one of them. The media endorses permissive public school education that is corrupting our youngsters. (Littleton is only the tip of the iceberg.)

The Church has its own schools which teach Godly virtues, the Ten Commandments and the Beatitudes. The media fights for homosexual lifestyles that most often include sodomy. Christ teaches through His Church that sodomy is the sin that brought down Sodom and Gomorrah. The media sides with pagan practices and highlights them (i.e., movie stars and college kids living together). The Church teaches virginity outside of marriage. The media goes along with Planned Parenthood that teaches that artificial contraception, abortion, and homosexual unions are normal and are to be endorsed. The Church stands on God's law revealed in Nature and in Scripture.

The Church is, according to the Scriptures, "the pillar and standard of truth." (1Tim 3:15). The media is anything but, with the amount of innuendoes, half truths, and outright lies it prints. The Church endorses poverty, chastity, and obedience for everyone. The media endorses the opposite: money, sex, and power.

If it were "cover-up," they would attack "cover-up in all of its many forms," especially in the media itself. No, the issue is blatantly anti-Catholic. It is sowing these seeds of anti-Catholicism in the minds of Americans, especially in our youth. Such seeds of bigotry in the past have produced the Holocaust, the horrendous slaughter of Catholics and Protestants in northern Ireland, and the situation in Israel today. George Santayana said, in his wisdom, "Those who fail to learn from the lessons of history are doomed to repeat them."

All People of Good Will

To Fight Bigotry in all Forms

If this were happening to my Jewish brothers and sisters, I would be at your side. It is not, however. It is against us and you need to stand strongly at our side. If this were happening to my black brothers and sisters, I would voice my concern as I did with Martin Luther King, Jr. If this were happening to my Protestant brothers and sisters, I would fight just as strongly against such bias. It is happening to the Church I love and the priesthood that I have served since 1948 when I first entered the seminary.

We Need Your Help

So I am asking everyone to join with me to see bigotry for what it is. I am asking you to reach out in love and forgiveness to your Catholic brothers and sisters who are being so persecuted.

A Strong Word to the Media

And I would strongly say to the media of America that you are absolutely and definitely wrong to stand for bigotry. History will prove you wrong. Slander and defamation of character are never God's way or the American way. It is evil. It is an abomination. It is wrong. I would say to everyone — Catholic, Muslim, Jew, or Protestant — you are not a good Catholic if you are bigoted against Muslims, Jews, or Protestants, and an even worse American; if you are Protestant and your Protestantism gives you recourse to bias and bigotry, you are not a good Protestant or a good American; if you are a Jew and your jewishness allows you to be bigoted against Catholics or Protestants, you are neither a good Jew nor a loyal American.

A New Battlefield

For again we are in a great battlefield, testing to see if this nation or any nation so conceived and so dedicated can long endure. Bigotry and bias will always divide us. We cannot allow it to come to or remain in any group. Bias is not Jewish. Bigotry is not Christian. And neither bias nor bigotry are American. I call out to the good people in the media who, like John Leo, are saying, "The news media are damaging their honesty and credibility." I call upon all my fellow Americans of every race, religion, or color to stand with your Catholic brothers who are being painted with a broad negative brush and to say to the media, "Enough is enough. In the name of God and decency and in the name of our founding fathers, it has to cease!" Too much damage has been done. You must repent and come back to the highest ideas of our land. It has to cease. For the sake of the American experiment, it has to cease.

For the fruit of bigotry and hatred is violence; the fruit of violence is terrorism; and fruit of terrorism is war. As Mother Teresa said, "The fruit of prayer is love, the fruit of love is peace."

Long ago St Francis said, "Where there is hatred, let me sow love; where there is injury, pardon."

19
God's Judgment on our Land

Upon Cracking Rocks

The foundations of America are no longer solid rocks cemented in its Judaic-Christian heritage. They have become brittle, crumbling under the weight of sin. The landscape of our history once great is in moral decay.

Civilizations Crumble from Within

Tolstoy, the great historian, tells us that of the 21 civilizations that have come and gone, 19 have decayed from within. The last was the great Roman Empire that conquered most of the known Mediterranean world of its day. Even while it romped in apparent power and prosperity, its foundations were crumbling beneath it, so Gibbon told us in his great book, *The Rise and Fall of the Roman Empire.*

Rome was founded upon high moral standards. Each father was respected as the head of the home and had legal authority to discipline his children. Education was the prime responsibility of the parents. This further strengthened the children's honor and respect for their parents and also deepened the communication and understanding between parents and children. Strong Roman families produced a strong Roman nation. Great building programs began in Rome. A vast network of highways united the Empire. Magnificent public buildings, coliseums and amphitheaters were constructed. As families prospered, many parents hired educated Greeks to teach their children. Greek philosophy with its godless and humanistic base entered unchecked into Roman children. Women demanded more rights. New marriage contracts were designed, including open marriages. Pornography and the worship of the body infiltrated into the Roman baths. Homosexuality began to be accepted.

By the first century AD, fathers had lost their legal authority.

Authority was given to the village, then to the city, then to the state, and finally to the Empire. Big government could not solve housing shortages, polluted air, crime in the streets, high cost of living, and soaring rents. Unemployment became a gigantic problem so the government created a multitude of civil servant jobs including building inspectors, health inspectors and tax collectors. Rome was tolerant of all false religious practices. Christians alone were persecuted and thrown to the lions, for by their very nature, Christians were for strong families, the headship of fathers, the sanctity of the home and parental rights. By the 3rd century, the glory that was Rome was a thing of the past. Christianity had conquered it.

The Civilization of Greece

Socrates, Plato and Aristotle were the greatest philosophers of their day. As Greek civilization rose to its golden age, we saw the first democracy, splendid architecture and excellence in culture. According to a popular proverb, there were more gods in Athens than men. But corruption crept into politics, business, personal life and even religion. Greece, too, fell because Greece did not have the moral fiber to defeat its own interior onslaught of immorality.

The Mayan Nation

Other great civilizations have come and gone. The Mayan nation developed brain surgery, built an incredible network of irrigation canals and excelled in mathematics and astronomy. Interior corruption set in. That great civilization has now come and gone.

America, You're Too Young to Die

For the past five decades, we have seen America go into decay. We've separated God from state and saw even the medical profession murder our unborn. We are reeling from epidemic proportions of abortions, sexually-transmitted diseases, pornography, divorce and sodomy. We are reaping what we have sown. The combined attempts of politicians, educators and sociologists are failing to provide any lasting solution. The American public has expressed its outrage at the growing problem of child abuse. Is such behavior really very surprising in a promiscuous society that promotes moral perversion on television, in movies, in music and in magazines; and where pornography is pumped wholesale into the living rooms of America?

Believing the Lie

"God shall send them strong delusion that they shall believe the lie" (2 Thes 2:11). When we listen to the lie, we dethrone God, His Church and His Bible, and we make man the center of everything.

We believe the lie:

When we exalt human reason above revelation,

When we trust science above God's principles,

When we believe that man is evolving of himself to greater perfection,

When we replace God's commandments with situation ethics,

When we reject the absolutes in favor of the relative,

When we exalt the subjective over the objective,

When we promote instant gratification over virtue, and

When we make the state sovereign and attack the Church.

A Nation Adrift

In April, 1912, the largest and strongest ocean liner, Titanic, set out on its maiden voyage. Everyone considered it unsinkable. But we all know it sank, claiming more than 1,500 lives. Less than 20 miles away was the Californian that could have come to its rescue, but the radio operator had fallen asleep on duty. Like the Titanic, our great ship of state has gone adrift, people have fallen asleep morally, and we are headed for a fateful collision. Many feel that we are unsinkable. The truth of the matter is, we are in grave danger.

God has given us the Church to alert our country of its danger. Our Holy Father has told us clearly what we must do. He has laid out for us a seven point plan in his great apostolic constitution entitled, As We Enter the Third Millennium.

First and foremost, he is calling us to holiness — to think and love and act like Jesus.

Second, he is calling us to a life of prayer, which he calls a conversation - that is, talking and listening to God as God speaks to us through his Word, his Church and the inward prophetic flow of insights and understandings that the Spirit puts into our minds and hearts. He has held up for us four great models of prayer: St. Catherine of Siena, St. John of the Cross, St. Teresa of Avila and St. Theresa the Little Flower.

Third, he is calling us to a deeper devotion to the Eucharist and to Eucharistic Adoration so that Christ may truly nurture our souls with great wisdom, holiness and love.

Fourth, he is calling us to frequent confession so that consciences may experience the cleansing power of Christ's blood.

Fifth, he is calling us to live by the Spirit with a real openness to all the charisms which he states are more necessary today than ever before.

Sixth, he is asking us to frequently meditate upon God's Word as revealed especially through the Scriptures and the new Catechism.

Seventh, he is calling us to a new evangelization so that we might bring the light of the Gospel to a darkened world that needs it desperately.

Section III
Strategies for a Nation
to be Born Anew

20
What September 11th Taught Us

The United States is not the same country that it was before Sept. 11th. This is self-evident to almost everyone. Our national pride as well as our economy has suffered. Air traffic is more difficult. Fewer people are traveling in general, and our lives are perceived as much more fragile. Many people have made an analysis of the events of that Tuesday never to be forgotten. This is a collection of some of their observations and thoughts, all of which come from *From the Ashes, A Spiritual Response on the Attack on America*, collected by the editors of Beliefnet/Rodale Book.

1. God glories in poor and ordinary people. "American culture glories in celebrity. People can be famous, it seems, simply for being famous, and the antics and opinions of celebrities have come to be considered legitimate news. But the events of Sept. 11th expose the shallowness of our preoccupation with fame. In a real crisis, people did not want to hear from movie stars. They were more likely to turn to the neighborhood clergy."

Suddenly, the heroes were fire fighters, police officers and rescue workers and so many thousands of people willing to lend a hand. Suddenly, ordinary lives emerged from our cellophaned artificiality, and the real heroes were millions of ordinary people. Jesus favored ordinary people. Mary, his mother, Joseph, his foster father, and all of his apostles and disciples and followers were then, as now, ordinary people. Obviously, God glories in poor and ordinary people. Hopefully, it is a lesson we will cling to." By Kathleen Norris, author of *The Cloister Walk and Amazing Grace*.

2. We all should live more simply. This lesson first preached

by the prophets, by Jesus and by people like Mother Teresa and St. Francis came home to us after that fateful Tuesday. "American culture thrives on the promotion of material things. But after Sept. 11, the voices hawking current fashions, the latest prescription drugs, the top-of-the-line appliances, and technological wonders were silenced. With remarkable disregard for the bottom line, television executives shoved advertisements aside and kept the news coming. Corporate executives agreed, recognizing that commercials would seem callous under the circumstances and, for a few days, the distraction of advertising was blessedly absent from our lives. We did not have to listen to anyone exalt over a stain remover, a bathroom cleanser, or a new car, as if these products were of genuine importance in our lives. During that famous week, it was easy to remember that relationships with other people matter far more than things." From Kathleen Norris, "God Was Where God Chose To Be," an article from *From the Ashes, a Spiritual Response to the Attack on America*.

3. We should promote a culture of peace. "American culture promotes the imagery of violence, even as it seeks to ignore the effects of real violence on people's lives. Action-film actors are cartoon figures surviving gun battles, auto accidents, fire, falls, and explosions that would kill an ordinary mortal. Death is entertainment, especially when it's mostly the bad guys who die. But now that the death of so many innocent people has been forced into our consciousness, we will do well to recall our own mortality in a meaningful way. The suggestion St. Benedict made over 1,500 years ago, to 'Keep death daily before your eyes,' can be a spiritual tool that helps us to value life and those we share it with. Let petty disagreements go, kiss your wife or husband good-bye, send your kids off to school with a word of encouragement rather than complaint. It may be an ordinary Tuesday morning, but it is also precious time, because life doesn't last forever." By Kathleen Norris, author of *The Cloister Walk and Amazing Grace*.

4. Americans have a love-hate relationship with religion. "Many people explain themselves as 'spiritual' but not 'religious,'

implying that institutional religion has no place in their lives. But during the week of September 11, we turned on our televisions and saw Americans at prayer, in churches and cathedrals, in mosques, synagogues, and ashrams. The old religious traditions and sacred spaces had something to offer us after all in our hour of need. The truth is that these communities of faith were there all along, and will still be there after the present crises has passed. But in the clutter of American life, the loud culture of argument, we simply could not see them, or hear their messages of good will.

"In the world revealed to us during the week of September 11, religion has a legitimate place, and recognizing this is especially important in light of the appalling distortion of Islam that led to the terrorist attacks. We need not remain mired in bitterness, assuming that God somehow caused these horrible acts to take place. 'Where was God?'

Is a question that naturally arises whenever we are faced with terrible loss. On the morning of September 11, I believe that God was where God has chosen to be, nailed to a cross, constructed by human beings." By Kathleen Norris, author of *The Cloister Walk* and *Amazing Grace.*

5. We love best when we are broken. "For me, the belief that God suffers with us helps explain the fact that disaster so often brings out our strengths. As I wrote in my book, *Amazing Grace*, in a chapter on the word 'apocalypse,' 'We human beings learn best how to love when we're a bit broken, when plans fall apart, when our myths of self-sufficiency and safety are shattered. Apocalypse is meant to bring us to our senses, allowing us a sober if painful glimpse of what is possible in the new life we build from the ashes of the old.'

"It is a difficult task that is set before use, but it helps to realize that in the world revealed by apocalypse, destruction does not have the last word. It is hope that emerges, inviting us to believe that, despite considerable evidence to the contrary, it is not evil that prevails, but the good. If this seems far-fetched, hopelessly pie-in-the-sky, we have only to recall the firemen, police officers, medical personnel, and chaplains of New York City, who, when confronted with unthinkable evil, chose the good. In the hope of bring-ing aid and comfort to people who were strangers to them, they gave up their lives. In the Christian tradition, there is no greater good than this." By Kathleen Norris, author of *The Cloister Walk* and *Amazing Grace*.

6. God will make a way for redemption. Throughout the Scrip-tures, God always makes a way. He is there as our deliverer, our redeemer, our savior. Listen to Max Lucado's prayer.

"We are sad, Father. For as the innocent are buried, our inno-cence is buried as well. We thought we were safe. Perhaps we should have known better. But we didn't.

"And so we come to you. We don't ask you for help; we beg you for it. We don't request it; we implore it. We know that you can do. We've read the accounts. We've pondered the stories and now we plead, 'Do it again, Lord. Do it again.'

"Remember Joseph? You rescued him from the pit. You can do the same for us. Do it again, Lord.

"Remember the Hebrews in Egypt? You protected their chil-dren from the angel of death. We have children, too, Lord. Do it again.

"And Sarah? Remember her prayers? You heard them. Joshua? Remember his fears? You inspired him. The women at the tomb? You resurrected their hope. The doubts of Thomas? You took them away. Do it again, Lord. Do it again.

"You changed Daniel from a captive into a king's counselor. You took Peter the fisherman and made him Peter and apostle. Because of you, David went from leading sheep to leading armies. Do it again, Lord, for we need counselors today, Lord. We need apostles. We need leaders. Do it again, dear Lord.

"Most of all, do again what you did at Calvary. What we saw here that Tuesday, you saw there that Friday. Innocence slaugh-tered. Goodness murdered. Mothers weeping. Evil dancing. Just as the ash fell on our children, the darkness fell on your Son. Just as our towers were shattered, the very Tower of Eternity was pierced.

"And by dusk, heaven's sweetest song was silent, buried be-hind a rock.

"But you did not waver, O Lord. You did not waver. After 3 days in a dark hole, you rolled the rock and rumbled the earth and turned the darkest Friday into the brightest Sunday. Do it again, lord. Grant us a September Easter.

"We thank you, dear Father, for these hours of unity. Christians are praying with Jews. Republicans are standing with Democrats. Skin colors have been covered by the ash of burning buildings. We thank you for these hours of unity.

"And we thank you for these hours of prayer. The Enemy sought to bring us to our knees and succeeded. He had no idea, however, that we would kneel before you. And he has no idea what you can do.

"Let your mercy be upon our president, vice president, and their families. Grant to those who lead us wisdom beyond their years and experience. Have mercy upon the souls who have departed and the wounded who remain. Give us grace that we might forgive and faith that we might believe.

"And look kindly upon your church. For 2,000 years you've used her to heal a hurting world.

"Do it again, Lord. Do it again.

"Through Christ, Amen."

Written by Max Lucado, pastor of Oak Hills Church of Christ in San Antonio, Texas, and a Christian author of more than 25 books.

7. God gives us freedom to choose the good because He is a God of love. God could have created a world without freedom, a world without love, a pre-determined world where everything and everyone would react either by nature or by instinct. In fact, the world He created is, to a large extent, a predetermined world. A star must shine, a fish must swim, a dog must bark. But because God is love, He wanted to share the ability to love with some of His creation. And so He gave mankind freedom. This is the great answer to the evil in the world.

"How could a good God have allowed such massive evil? No question poses a greater stumbling block to Christian faith; no question is more difficult for Christians to answer. Yet the biblical worldview does give us a good answer.

"The simple answer to why bad things happen to so-called good people is that God loved us so much that he made us free moral agents in his image. He designed creatures with the ability to make choices, to choose either good or evil. The original humans, Adam and Eve, exercised that choice — and chose to disobey God. In doing so, they rejected God's good, thus creating sin and opening the door to death and evil.

"What happened last week was raw, naked evil—committed by men who made evil choices. But it was something else as well: It was merely a consequence of the fact that there is sin in the world. God could erase the consequences of sin immediately. But then we'd no longer be free moral agents; we would be robots. For without consequences, there is not real choice. God cannot simultaneously offer us free choice and then compel one choice over another—which is what would happen if he stopped all evil.

"Jesus himself was asked why bad things happen to good people. In Luke 13, we read that people asked him if the Galileans who were killed while worshipping at the altar were worse sinners than anyone else. "No," Jesus answered. And then he added, "Unless you repent you will all likewise perish." Jesus then reinforced his point. Recently, a tower in a nearby city had fallen; 18 people had been crushed to death. Jesus said, "Do you think that they were worse offenders than all the others who dwelt in Jerusalem? I tell you, no; but unless you repent you will all likewise perish." From "God Made Us Moral Agents," by Chuck Colson, founder of Prison Fellowship Ministries, taken from Breakpoint www.breakpoint.org.

8. September 11th united the world with us. "There has been a tremendous international response to our tragedy. When we were seen as vulnerable, the nations of the world responded especially since citizens of many nations perished at the World Trade Center. The world wept with us. We saw our national anthem played at Buckingham Palace where thousands prayed and wept with us. We saw school children in Asia at their desk with heads bowed in silence. We saw the crowds gathered at the Brandenburg Gate in

Germany paying respects to those who had died. We saw people in Australia and Israel and France and Spain with tear-stained faces and hands lifted in prayer. We saw the crowds at St. Peter's in Rome. And we came to realize that many in the world, more perhaps that we had expected, were indeed our friends." From *From the Ashes, A Spiritual Response to the Attack on America*, pg. 262-264.

9. What good can come from this evil?
"Perhaps even more amazing has been the constant counterpoint that has often become the dominant theme: that from this evil, good will come. President Bush affirmed this truth, stating that the intended goal of the terrorists will fail; that the United States will emerge united, stronger, and better after this carnage. Again and again the belief that good will come from this evil has been repeated by public officials, commentators, rescue workers, and ordinary citizens.

"What good can come from this evil? The fact that we are asking this question is in itself a tremendous benefit. Every one of us faces problems and difficulties in our lives, some minor and some life-threatening. Because we have heard this axiom so often in the light of the tragedies of that week, people today more than ever are confronting their own life situations, asking, 'What good can come from this?' What a tremendous shift of paradigms!

"I asked a group of fifth and sixth-grade children, 'What good has come from this evil?' 'People are more generous,' they replied. On television they had seen the professional rescue workers joined by volunteers, even though it meant they were risking their lives. The children were aware of the many ways people were working together to aid the victims and their families and the countless others whose lives were impacted in New York and Washington. But they had also told me that people around them had become more helpful and generous. Was their observation correct? Yes! Several studies by psychologists have uniformly documented that people observing someone being a good Samaritan were more likely to help another person they saw in need. A carefully crafted, groundbreaking study by psychologist Jon Haidt found that spectators who simply observed someone helping another received feelings of 'elevation.' What we have seen in the wake of recent terrorism bears this out.

"People have had strong feelings of anger, hurt, sorrow, and grief because of the carnage. At the same time, in response to seeing the selfless acts and heroism of many, people have experienced feelings of elevation. The observation of the children was accurate. People across the nation are being both more generous and more helpful and feeling better. The cruel acts of terrorists have had the unexpected result of creating a kinder, more caring American populace.

"Suddenly things have been put in a different perspective. As we have listened to reports of the last conversations from the hijacked planes or the Twin Towers, we have been reminded of the importance of families. Not just the families of the victims. We have been jolted to a new awareness of the importance of our own families. Even when we knew our family members were not in any of the cities where the destruction had reigned, we felt it was important to call. A teen told me he was aware that those in his home had become more sensitive, more caring. Parents were trying to find the words to explain the events to their children. For many, this was the first serious conversation families have had for a long time. Sometimes words failed, and the family members were silent—but there was a togetherness in their silence. One mother told me, 'We sat on the floor, just holding hands and praying. It's the first time we have done that.'

"A nurse in the cardiac intensive care unit observed a difference. Usually many of the heart patients are in denial about the seriousness of their condition, but as they watched the continuing coverage on television they were impressed with the suddenness of life and death. Patients with tears in their eyes began to deal honestly with their own mortality in a healthy way, speaking openly with the medical staff about their concerns, rearranging their priorities, and accepting the necessary change in regimen.

"Outside the hospital, ordinary folks in every walk of life report that they have new feelings of thanksgiving for life itself. No longer taken for granted, each day is viewed as a gift, and individuals are discovering the joy of grateful living.

"In villages and cities across America there are new feelings of community. Many people told me that neighbors are talking to neighbors with whom they never passed the time of day. In the office, people who were barely acquaintances are showing concern for each other. Neighborhoods are pulling together. There is a new sense of camaraderie. Flags are being flown from houses and on autos. Candlelight vigils are being held. Donors spend hours in line to give blood.

"There has been a new national unity. Democrats and Republicans are working together in a common cause. People at every level are pulling together. Despite frequent warnings that the war against terrorists may be long and require sacrifice, the response of people in general is that Americans do better in hard times. In the face of the prospect of fewer material advantages, they see a return to the more basic moral and spiritual values.

"Americans are a religious people, with the overwhelming majority professing faith in God. During this time of national emergency, the houses of worship have been filled. Those in grief have found solace and comfort in faith. Others have found strength and courage to face an uncertain future. And it has not only been individuals and communities of faith that have turned to religion. In a real sense it has been a national response. The nation watched as the leaders of the country gathered in the National Cathedral for an ecumenical service. Billy Graham and other religious leaders sounded a call to righteousness as well as the benefits of trust in Almighty God. A National Day of Prayer was observed. Clergy of all faiths were prominent in the news coverage. Many believe this may be the beginning of the turning of a nation from materialism to a new spirituality.

By The Rev. William D. Webber, Baptist pastor for 40 years and author of *A Rustle of Angels*.

10. We are humbled and holier. From *God Still Answers Prayers* by Bruce Wilkinson: "Are goodness and hope and God to be found in the ashes? I believe so. Certainly, for those most

directly affected, it may be too soon to believe any answers or to receive any comfort. But I believe that answers and comfort will come. As a nation, we've only begun to emerge from the shock, and the grief and loss will be with us for years. Yet for every life lost, we're already seeing thousands upon thousands of acts of heroism and generosity.

"These are times that strip away the places, feelings, routines, and assumptions that had seemed most real to us and had been most often the measure of our wealth. We're left feeling impoverished, vulnerable, and perhaps abandoned by God. Feeling, in other words, utterly mortal.

These are times when we turn to prayer. And in that turning I find great hope. My friend Max Lucado wrote recently, 'This is a different country than it was a week ago. We're not as self-centered as we were. We're not as self-reliant as we were. Hands are out. Knees are bent. This is not normal. And I have to ask the question, 'Do we want to go back to normal?' Perhaps the best response to this tragedy is to refuse to go back to normal.'

"I agree with Max. In fact, these are times when 'normal' living and real prayer flourish best. Each time we sing 'God Bless America,' the nation is crying out for God's blessings and favor and help. Though we might wish them to be, God's blessings are not an insurance policy against the sufferings and tragedies that exist in our fallen world. The Apostle Peter advised, 'Do not think it strange concerning the fiery trial which is to try you, as though some strange thing happened to you' (1 Peter 4:12).

"But the experience of such pain doesn't mean we aren't also able to experience God's blessings. When we're in the midst of these sufferings, our Heavenly Father longs to pour out his supernatural favor on all who are willing to ask. If ever people from all walks of life sense a need for divine aid and blessing, it is now.

"For Christians who are sensing a new readiness to live out their faith, this is a most promising moment. By God's grace and power, now is the time to step up to a larger life of ministry and impact for eternity. Jesus' passion was that his disciples would bless the whole world—people of every race and creed and circumstance. Our passion can be for nothing less.

"That's why it's so heartening to see churches, communities, and individuals rising to incredible feats of service. And as we stretch beyond our comfort zones in God's service, we discover that his hand is available to empower us. I recall an example from the Old Testament of how God works through us in desperate times. Many years after Jerusalem had been left in ruins by enemy forces, it fell to a man named Zerubbabel to lead in the effort to rebuild the city. When he balked at the task, God reminded him that he would succeed 'not by might nor by power, but by My Spirit.' Therefore, I encourage Christians everywhere to pray boldly, not only for significant ministry in Jesus' name but also for the power of the Spirit to accomplish it."

11. Life is fragile. A sermon by the Rev. Bill Hybels. "Deep inside all of us there's a subconscious awareness that our lives are quite precarious. Deep down we know disease can strike and accidents can happen, unforeseen events can interrupt our carefully planned lives. Bad things might happen to other people. We're pretty sure we're insulated . . . they won't happen to us. And when we live calamity-free for long periods of time, not only do we feel a kind of invincibility, but we slowly begin to take life itself for granted. We stop thanking God for the gift of it—for the daily blessedness of it. We stop thanking God for sunrises and sunsets and for spring rains and fall colors. In a way we get too accustomed to the privilege of living, until a day like Tuesday comes.

"Joe Ditmar, a Chicago business guy, was on the 105th story of the World Trade Center when the terrorists strike began. He was fortunate enough to find his way out just before the building collapsed. In an interview with the press he kept saying, 'I will never, ever take life for granted again.' See, he came very close to the alternative. Each day since Tuesday he's been looking at nature differently, people differently, his faith differently, and especially he's been looking at his family differently. He was quoted as saying that when he was running for his life, he just had that image of his family in front of his face and he was running to them with all of his might. This guy's pretty thankful just for life this weekend.

"Did you notice in all these cell phone calls that were made from hijacked airplanes and burning buildings in the final moments of someone's life. . .I mean, when the alternate to life was near, you know what most folks did with those last gasps of breath they had? They just said, 'I love you. I love you. Tell Dad. Tell Mom. Tell the kids.' There's a learning in this, friends. Life is fragile. Life is relatively brief against the backdrop of eternity. It's a scandalously gracious gift from the hand of a good God. A gift that should be sincerely celebrated each day by those of us whose hourglass still contains some grains of sand. And what better way to celebrate this gift than by carrying out the instruction of the giver of the gift who said, 'If you love God with all your heart, soul, mind, and strength. . .' If you love others, family and friends, you will experience the gift of life in all its fullness. There's a lesson in this for us. A lesson about this glorious gift of life."

12. Life is warfare against evil. From a sermon by the Rev. Bill Hybels: "Evil is alive and well. Need we spend much time on this one, really? When times are peaceful and crime rates are falling and circumstances have been kind to us, we sometimes get lulled into forgetting that there's a ferocious battle being fought in this cosmos; a battle between the forces of good and evil. The Bible teaches from cover to cover that this spiritual war that's going on between the forces of good and evil is real. It's not folklore. It's not some religious fantasy idea. It's real. The Bible tells us that this battle goes on, that it's fought on the battlefields of individuals' minds and hearts. And the Bible teaches that the outcome of these individual battles between good and evil will have enormous impact on a society.

"In recent days, we've all had front row seats to what happens when the tide of the battle goes in the favor of evil forces. Unimaginable deeds are done. Tuesday morning in my office, as I and my son and a few friends were watching thousands of innocent people being burned and crushed, the thought happened into my mind that quite possibly in another office somewhere on the other side of the world the instigators of this carnage are high-fiving one another, breaking out the champagne and saying, "We did it. We did it."

and when that thought came into my mind, I almost got physically ill. I remember thinking, if that happened, it's as evil as evil can be. But the man of the station of evil is not limited to the relatively small group of people who planned this. What about all the accomplices who have been taking money for these past few years helping these few pull this off? That's pretty evil. What about people in various parts of the world who broke out in dancing and partying in the streets when they saw the television coverage of this catastrophe, rejoicing in the bloodshed of innocent people? I'd call that evil. And what about the gas station owners right here in the U.S., right here in the state of Illinois, who doubled and tripled their gasoline prices to profiteer from the slaughter of fellow Americans? That qualifies as evil in my book. And then what about the frustrated and angry Americans whose tempers boiled over and started accosting and assaulting innocent Arab-Americans, dragging them out of cabs, beating them, throwing Molotov cocktails into their homes and places of worship?"

13. God's kingdom turns us upside down, or rather right side up. "Some scholars refer to it as the 'kingdom inversion principle.' I sometimes call it the 'winning through losing principle.' It pertains to how God manages to produce something out of good even when the most difficult circumstances are what cause you to know this activity in the first place. I want to be very clear about this — no thinking person could attribute Tuesday's actions to the hand of a good God. God did not author what happened on Tuesday. God was repulsed by it. God stood and watched people whom he created, in whom he invested a free will; he watched them make decisions that broke his heart. But then, in the middle of this horrendous catastrophe, God moved into action in curious, behind-the-scenes ways, and he's been working and he's been creating something that we need to notice and wonder about. . .

"Let me just come right out and say it. Last Tuesday we suffered a terrible, national defeat. We lost two times the number of lives that we did on Pearl Harbor day. We lost a collective sense of security that may never be regained in our land. We lost face before a watching world. As one newspaper put it, 'America the invincible became America the vulnerable.' But what did our loss evoke in our citizens and our people since last Tuesday? Let me ask that another way. What has God been raising up out of the rubble on the eastern seaboard? What kind of work has God been up to against the backdrop of that horrendous loss?

"Well, first, we've seen unforgettable acts of heroism. Friends, I will never look at a firefighter the same way the rest of my life. Hundreds of them running toward the burning inferno instead of away from it; running up the steps of the Trade Center while people are racing for their lives coming down. And they're in there trying to save people they don't even know and they're not going to get a bonus for it. They were stirred to do something that defies human logic; to overcome the fear that would be in play in each of our lives were we in their shoes. Their bravery becomes part of our collective national legacy. It lifts us up as a people. Their bravery dignifies all of us. It's God at work, friends. The same could be said of police officers and other rescue workers. And what about the airplane passengers who used their cell phones to figure out that the hijackers were probably headed for Camp David or the Capitol or the White House? As best the story can be pieced together, these passengers stormed the cockpit where the hijackers were, they drove the plane into the ground to their own deaths in order to avert a greater tragedy." From "Processing a National Tragedy," a sermon by Rev. Bill Hybels, pastor of Willow Creek Community Church, South Barrington, Illinois.

14. Forgiveness must overcome — It's God's Way. "One of those killed in Manhattan was a fellow pastor and close friend of mine. A true man of God, Father Mychal Judge was killed while administering last rites to a fireman injured during the rescue effort. Through Father Mychal and the hundreds of police, firefighters, and other rescue workers who lost their lives while helping others, the words of Jesus have become newly alive: 'No greater service can a man do than to lay down his life for his friend.'

"Father Mychal's service was not limited to New York. Over the last years he traveled to Northern Ireland three times with me and our mutual friend, New York Police Department detective

Steven McDonald, to spread a message of reconciliation there. We were planning a similar trip to Israel this October.

"In these places torn by years of violence, Steven, shot in the line of duty by a teenage and paralyzed from the neck down, would tell people, 'The only thing worse than a bullet in my spine would have been to nurture revenge in my heart. Such an attitude would only have extended my tragic injury into my soul, further hurting my wife, son, and others. It is bad enough that the physical effects are permanent, but at least I can choose to prevent spiritual injury.'

"At Steven's side, Father Mychal said, 'When peace comes to this country, and it will come some day, there will be memories, there will be families that were torn apart. Forgiveness is a tremendously long, ongoing process and it needs great grace and strength from above. I have my own problems, my own hates, my own harsh feelings; I am as human as anybody else. So I have to have this ongoing forgiveness in my heart, too." From *Is Forgiveness Possible*, by Johann Christopher Arnold, Bruderhof Community pastor, author of *Why Forgive*.

21
May God Heal Our Nation

What Happens When a Nation Repents?

God has given to us the great story of the city-state of Nineveh, the capital of mighty Assyria, which at that time was mightier than Babylon. God sent Jonah, the reluctant prophet, to tell the city to repent. "Yet forty days and Nineveh shall be overthrown" (Jonah 3:4). To Jonah's amazement, the people believed God, proclaimed a fast and put on sackcloth — from the greatest to the least. Even the king began to cry unto God and asked for the grace of repentance. God promptly restored a repentant nation and granted a delay in the city's predicted destruction — in that case 160 years. Those who repented and many of their descendants were spared the destruction that finally came in 612BC.

What Happens When a Nation Does Not Repent?

Nineveh began to backslide. Surrounding nations were corrupted and began to influence the citizens of Nineveh. Lust, greed and immorality overtook it, and Nineveh was so totally destroyed that not a single person remained there. In fact, for hundreds of years it laid undiscovered, leading many to believe that the Nineveh story was only a myth.

Repent for the Kingdom of God Is at Hand

The call to repentance is one of the most consistent themes of both the old and new testaments. Moses called for it, as did Joshua, John the Baptist and, of course, Jesus. The Christian Church still preaches it. America, however, has lost its sense of sin. Carl Menninger's startling book, *Whatever Became of Sin*, is the most timely question in the United States today. The human heart, devoid of God's Spirit, can turn to evil beyond all words.

Christ the Only Savior

Jesus Christ has given to us the Church with its Magisterium to be the pillar and standard of truth. And through the Church, He has given us the new Catechism, which clearly maps out the road that we must follow. Through His Church, He has given us a priesthood, a sacramental system, Eucharistic Adoration, devotion to the Sacred Heart and all the spiritual helps we need to transform our lives. He is sending His mother all over the world to tell us to return to her Son and to follow her hand-picked pope, John Paul II. But we must listen, we must repent.

22
"If My People Will Humble Themselves and Pray, I will Heal Their Land" (2 Chron 7:14)

God's Promise

God has promised us in the Scriptures that "If my people who are called by my name will humble themselves and pray and seek my face, I will hear from Heaven. I will restore the nation and heal their land." (2Chron 7:14) This is an amazing promise proven in all the Scriptures. Whenever God's people are faithful to Him and obey His Commandments, God blesses them abundantly. One of the great blessings was that He restored them to peace and made their enemies to be at peace with them. Whenever they disobeyed, God allowed their enemies to overtake them.

Eight Unholy Years

The United States of America towards the end of the twentieth century went through eight unholy years under a president and vice president who were open to abortion (even partial birth abortion) were soft on pornography and stressed the separation of God from state. Federal prosecutions for hard core pornography plummeted from 42 in 1992 to just six in 1997. Even those numbers are misleading. Many of the people convicted during this sin-filled administration actually made plea-bargaining agreements that kept them from been tried for more serious crimes, including child pornography. In 1993, pornography was a $3.9 billion per year industry, soon to become more than a $10 billion a year industry. As one porn executive put it, "The President is a total supporter of the pornography industry. He's always been on our team." Our media are now filled with violence, vulgarity, pornography and promiscuity.

A Return to God

Presently under a God-fearing President, we have seen a major turnaround. We have an administration that is pro-God, pro-family, and pro-life. His faith and integrity have been even more visible since the tragedies of September 11th of this year. He has led the whole country back to prayer. From the White House to the Capitol, from the Senate floor to Ground Zero, from the Pentagon to Yankee Stadium, our country has been at prayer. *God Bless America* is boldly sung throughout our land. Two great things have happened in the soul of America. We are now a grieving nation at prayer, and we are united in our resolve to rid the world of evil people who attack our way of life.

We Must Go Deeper

Most Americans realize that the solution lies deeper than diplomacy or military might. As Benjamin Franklin said long ago, "God governs in the affairs of men. Unless the Lord builds the house, they labor in vain that build it." America is returning to God in her resolve to make this a nation under God once again.

God Bless America

God has indeed blessed America. Over the last 200 years—under His Providence—America has risen to levels and achievements attained by no other nation in the history of the world. Yet, ironically, in a nation once distinguished for its faith and made great by its people of faith, we have in recent years regressed to the point where public expressions of that traditional faith are now viewed as a threat to government. This is nowhere more evident than in our courts.

No Cross

For example, in the case Warsaw v. Tehachapi, a federal court ruled that it was unconstitutional for a public cemetery to have a planter in the shape of a cross, for—as the court explained—if someone were to view that cross, it could cause "emotional distress" and thus constitute "injury-in-fact."

No Bible

In the case Roberts v. Madigan, a federal court first ruled that a teacher at school could not be seen publicly with his own personal copy of the Bible and then ruled that a classroom library containing 237 books must remove from the library the two books which dealt with Christianity.

No Christian Need Apply

In the case Alexander v. Nacogdoches School District, an anti-drug speaker on the policy board of the national drug czar's office was prohibited by a federal court from delivering his anti-drug message to students in the Nacogdoches, Texas, school district. The reason? The judge pointed out that the speaker was also known as a Christian minister and thus was disqualified from delivering a secular anti-drug message that he had already delivered to over 3,000,000 students at thousands of public schools.

On the Downward Swing

In the case Commonwealth v. Chambers, a man was convicted and sentenced by a jury for taking an axe handle and brutally clubbing to death a 71-year-old woman in order to steal her social security check. Yet that jury's sentence was overturned because the prosecuting attorney—in a statement which lasted less than five seconds—had mentioned a Bible verse in the courtroom. For mentioning seven words from the Bible in the courtroom, the jury sentence of a man convicted of a brutal murder was set aside!

Is this how government is to operate? Does the decision to overturn that jury sentence actually constitute good government? If one examines 1 Timothy 1, 1 Peter 2, Romans 13, or a number of other Scriptures, God makes it clear that the purpose of government is to reward the righteous and to punish the wicked. Yet in this case, the wicked was protected, and the righteous was punished. That decision violates every Biblical standard for good government.

An Outcry for Good Government

Such decisions as this fuel the outcry for good government. However, the means of securing good government has been debated in America for over three centuries—with differing conclusions on how to achieve that goal.

For example, in the 1660s, when the people of Carolina were drafting their first state constitution, they sought help from political philosopher John Locke. Locke subsequently authored their 1669 constitution in the belief that good government would be secured through the enactment of good laws. Locke reasoned that if righteous laws were in the constitution, then no matter who was placed into office, he would always be bound by those righteous laws.

Good People and Good Laws

William Penn applied a dramatically different philosophy at about the same time when he established the government of Pennsylvania. While Penn did believe that good laws were necessary, he did not believe that a long state constitution filled with righteous laws would be the means of securing good government.

Penn understood that something more than good laws was necessary. He explained: "Governments, like clocks, go from the motion men give them . . .Wherefore governments rather depend upon men, than men upon governments. Let men be good, and the government cannot be bad. . . .But if men be bad, the government [will] never [be] good.

Penn understood that the quality of government depended not upon the goodness found in laws, but rather upon the goodness found in leaders. Penn continued: "I know some say, "Let us have good laws, and no matter for the men that execute them." But let them consider that though good laws do well, good men do better; for good laws may [lack] good men. . .but good men will never [lack] good laws, nor [allow bad] ones."

Indeed, wicked people simply do not obey righteous laws; it is not in their nature to do so, else America would have no murder or theft; for we have laws which prohibit both. Conversely, good people in office not only obey good laws but they will not allow bad ones.

Righteous People

Penn's approach is shown to be accurate not only by history but also by the Scriptures. For example, Proverbs 29:2 declares: "When the righteous rule, the people rejoice; when the wicked rule, the people groan."

The key to good government is found in the quality of the people who rule, not in the quality of the laws they pass. Our Founding Fathers understood this. Consequently, it is not surprising that their first governments reflected the Proverbs 29:2 approach.

The Declaration of Independence

On the day they signed the Declaration of Independence, the

Founding Fathers underwent an immediate transformation. The day before, each of them had been a British citizen, living in a British colony, with thirteen crown-appointed British state governments. However, when they signed that document and separated from Great Britain, they lost all of their state governments.

Not a Democracy

Our Founding Fathers had an opportunity to establish a democracy and chose not to; they specifically chose to establish a republic. In their minds, we were not—and were never to become—a democracy. Founding Father Fisher Ames declared: "A democracy is a volcano which conceals the fiery materials of its own destruction. These will produce an eruption, and carry desolation in their way."

Founding Father Benjamin Rush was equally pointed; he noted: "A simple democracy is the devil's own government."

Founding Father John Adams similarly stated: "Remember, democracy never lasts long. It soon wastes, exhausts, and murders itself. There never was a democracy yet that did not commit suicide."

So strongly did the Founders oppose a democracy that when they created the Constitution, they included a provision to keep America from becoming a democracy. Article 4, Section 4 of the Constitution requires that "each State maintain a republican form of government:—a "republican" form of government as opposed to a "democratic" one. That is, each was to function as a republic, not a democracy.

What, then, is the difference between a democracy and a republic? Noah Webster explained that difference. He told students: "{O}ur citizens should early understand that the genuine source of correct republican principles is the Bible, particularly the New Testament, or the Christian religion."

The difference between a republic and a democracy is the source of its authority.

In a democracy, whatever the people desire is what becomes policy. If a majority of the people decide that murder is no longer a crime, in a democracy, murder will no longer be a crime. However, not so in our republic. In our republic, murder will always be a crime, for murder is always a crime in the Word of God. It is this foundation which has given our republic such enduring stability; for since man does not change, he continues to need the same restraints he has always needed; it is the rights and wrongs revealed in the Bible which have provided those guidelines for our republic.

The Choice is Clear

The real terrorists are not simply those of the Middle East, but those who have, for three generations, been destroying the twin pillars of our country—religion and morality, as Washington said. The question of the hour is: Will we be, once again, a nation under God with our enemies at peace with us, or still under attack? From without, yes; but more fearfully, from within. Under God or under attack? The choice is clear.

23
Which Way America? Up or Down
A Return to Our Roots

When a person or civilization is at the precipice overlooking ruin, the most progressive way is backwards - away from the abyss. God raised up America to be a light of revelation for the world. Christopher Columbus said as he read the Scriptures that he felt illuminations from the Holy Spirit that he was founding a new Israel, a Christian Israel, to be a light of revelation to the nations.

America was founded upon Godly principles; to be exact, Christian principles. Constitutionally, we were given the highest ideals known to mankind.

From 1776 to 1962, we were, as a nation, pro-God, pro-Christianity, pro-family, pro-life, pro-decency, pro-freedom, and pro-the common good. Beginning in 1962, we began to throw away our sacred heritage. In 1962, we separated God from state and did something that was horrendously unconstitutional. We restricted our teachers and public school children to from participating in prayer, from learning about the Ten Commandments, and from the Judaic-Christian backdrop that formed the very basis of the American educational system as set up by our Founding Fathers. Every known moral problem began to escalate, not only among public schools student but in the nation as well. With the new secularist and liberal philosophy, the 'separation of Church and state' began to take root in the minds and hearts of the American public. Now promiscuity, prostitution, sodomy, pornography, obscenity, atheism, violence, murder, rape, and incest dominate our land.

Supreme Court Suppresses Religious Freedom

Anyone born after 1962 never knew the United States of America. Before then, we had prayer in every public school. Obscenity, pornography, prostitution, abortion, public sodomy was outlawed. Every public school student was taught the Ten Commandments and had public prayer in the classroom. At every graduation or baccalaureate, a priest, minister or rabbi led public prayer. There was a dress code for all students. There were no co-ed dorms. That was before *Playboy*, and *Hustler*. Most Americans were for protecting youth. In the new liberal culture, Littleton, Colorado is just the tip of the iceberg.

The Three Ps - Promiscuity, Pornography, and College Presidents

Promiscuity, pornography are rampant on our campuses, as college president after college president has compromised values. Co-ed dorms are the norm. Schools don't even push morality. The only norm is to practice safe sex, which is not safe at all, since condoms have been proven tremendously defective in preventing the transmission of sexually transmitted diseases, especially AIDS. Socially transmitted diseases among our youth are commonplace. SAT scores are down and suicides are up as we witness a youthful America without roots.

Five Rs

America is reveling in excesses, rolling in riches, rollicking in pleasures, revolting in morals, and rotting in sin.

Too Young to Die

We now hear that America is "too young to die." We are met on a great battlefield testing whether this nation or any nation so conceived on Christian principles can long endure.

A Great Warning

September 11th was a great warning. God allowed the double symbols of money and military power to be attacked, for no amount of money and no military force can restore America. The question of the hour is, "Will we continue to head toward the precipice of destruction, or will we turn back to God?" For the battle line is drawn - it is Christ or chaos. The choice is clear. God, His principles and the choice of life, or death and destruction.

Choose Life

Moses said it long ago, "See, I have set before you this day life and good, death and evil. If you obey the commandments of the Lord your God which I command you this day, by loving the Lord your God and walking in His ways and by keeping His commandments and His statutes and his ordinances, then you shall live and multiply and the Lord your God will bless you . . . I call heaven and earth to witness against you this day, that I have set before you life and death, blessing and curse; therefore choose life, that you and your descendents may live, loving the Lord your God, obeying his voice, and cleaving to him; for that means life to you" (Dt 30:15-20).

A Return to the Faith of Our Fathers

As a nation we must get on our knees and humbly pray in contrition, confession, and commitment so that we can return to the faith of our fathers. The crisis is as acute as it can get. The danger of the American dream failing is imminent. Time is running out. God's mercy is coming to an end. Something miraculous must happen in the soul of America right now before it is too late. The choice is clearer than ever - repent or perish. Revival or ruin. And the question of the hour is, "Which way America, to be or not to be?"

Our School Children Can Pray in Public Schools

Although it is not well known, our school children in public schools are allowed to pray, to do religious term papers, to ask religious questions, to form a Bible club, and even to pray at graduation. Our Supreme Court has made it most clear that there is a distinction between those religious activities that are "student initiated" and those that are "administration initiated." "Student initiated" religious activities are allowed. Administration initiated religious activities are not.

In fact, last year, there was prayer at more than 10,000 public school graduations - all, of course, initiated by the students themselves. There are also at present more than 11,000 Bible student groups meeting regularly in public high schools. Once again, each of these is lead by the students, themselves. The American Civil Liberties Union, however, still tries to intimidate school systems with law suits. The American Center for Law and Justice constantly wins because it is the law of the land that a student does not leave their religious convictions on the doorstep as they enter the school building.

Following is a list complied by Dave Roever of Ft. Worth, Texas that spell out students' religious rights that are guaranteed under the present laws of the United States.

Students' Bill of Rights
On a Public School Campus

I. THE RIGHT to Meet with Other Religious Students
The Equal Access Act allows students the freedom to meet on campus for the purpose of discussing religious issues.

II. THE RIGHT to Identify Your Religious Beliefs through Signs and Symbols.
Students are free to express their religious beliefs through signs and symbols.

III. THE RIGHT to Talk about Your Religious Beliefs on Campus.

Freedom of speech is a fundamental right mandated in the Constitution and does not exclude the school yard.

IV. THE RIGHT to Distribute Religious Literature on Campus.

Distributing literature on campus may not be restricted simply because it is religious.

V. THE RIGHT to Pray on Campus.

Students may pray alone or with others so long as it does not disrupt school activities or is not forced on others.

6. THE RIGHT to Carry or Study Your Bible on Campus.

The Supreme Court has said that only state directed Bible reading is unconstitutional.

VII. THE RIGHT to Do Research Papers, Speeches, and Creative Projects with Religious Themes.

The First Amendment does not forbid all mention of religion in public schools.

VIII. THE RIGHT to Be Exempt.

Students may be exempt from activities and class content that contradict their religious beliefs.

IX. THE RIGHT to Celebrate or Study Religious Holidays on Campus.

Music, art, literature, and drama that have religious themes are permitted as part of the curriculum for school activities if presented in an objective manner as a traditional part of the cultural and religious heritage of the particular holiday.

X. THE RIGHT to Meet with School Officials.

The First Amendment to the Constitution forbids Congress to make any law that would restrict the right of the people to petition the Government (school officials).

24
A Pastoral Message:
Living With Faith and Hope After September 11
U.S. Conference of Catholic Bishops

November 14, 2001
Blessed are they who mourn,
    for they will be comforted....
Blessed are they who hunger and thirst for righteousness,
    for they will be satisfied.
Blessed are the merciful,
    for they will be shown mercy....
Blessed are the peacemakers,
    for they will be called children of God.
             (Mt 5:4,6,7,9)

These words of Jesus challenge us and offer us hope today as our community of faith responds to the terrible events of September 11 and their aftermath. As Catholic Bishops, we offer words of consolation, criteria for moral discernment, and a call to action and solidarity in these troubling and challenging times.

After September 11, we are a wounded people. We share loss and pain, anger and fear, shock and determination in the face of these attacks on our nation and all humanity. We also honor the selflessness of firefighters, police, chaplains, and other brave individuals who gave their lives in the service of others. They are true heroes and heroines.

In these difficult days, our faith has lifted us up and sustained us. Our nation turned to God in prayer and in faith with a new intensity. This was evident on cell phones on hijacked airliners, on stairways in doomed towers, in cathedrals and parish churches, at ecumenical and interfaith services, in our homes and hearts. Our faith teaches us about good and evil, free will and responsibility. Jesus' life, teaching, death and resurrection show us the meaning of love and justice in a broken world. Sacred Scripture and traditional ethical principles define what it means to make peace. They provide moral guidance on how the world should respond justly to terrorism in order to reestablish peace and order.

The events of September 11 were unique in their scale, but they were not isolated. Sadly, our world is losing respect for human life. Those who committed these atrocities do not distinguish between ordinary civilians and military combatants, and there is the threat of possible terrorist use of chemical, biological and nuclear weapons in the future.

The dreadful deeds of September 11 cannot go unanswered. We continue to urge resolve, restraint and greater attention to the roots of terrorism to protect against further attacks and to advance the global common good. Our nation must continue to respond in many ways, including diplomacy, economic measures, effective intelligence, more focus on security at home, and the legitimate use of force.

In our response to attacks on innocent civilians, we must be sure that we do not violate the norms of civilian immunity and proportionality. We believe every life is precious whether a person works at the World Trade Center or lives in Afghanistan. The traditional moral norms governing the use of force still apply, even in the face of terrorism on this scale.

No grievance, no matter what the claim, can legitimize what happened on September 11. Without in any way excusing indefensible terrorist acts, we still need to address those conditions of poverty and injustice which are exploited by terrorists. A successful campaign against terrorism will require a combination of resolve to do what is necessary to see it through, restraint to ensure that we act justly, and a long term focus on broader issues of justice and peace.

In these brief reflections, we seek to articulate traditional Catholic teaching as a guide for our people and nation, offering a moral framework, rather than a series of specific judgments on rapidly changing events. We believe our faith brings consolation, insight and hope in these challenging days.

Confronting Terrorism

The war-like acts of September 11 were appalling attacks on

our nation, our citizens and citizens of many other countries. The Holy Father rightly called these acts crimes against humanity. Terrorism is not a new problem, but this terrorist threat is unique because of its global dimensions and the sheer magnitude of the terror its authors are willing and able to unleash. It is also new for us because we have not experienced war-like acts of violence on our own soil for many decades.

The role of religion

We are particularly troubled that some who engage in and support this new form of terror seek to justify it, in part, as a religious act. Regrettably, the terrorists' notion of a religious war is inadvertently reinforced by those who would attribute the extremism of a few to Islam as a whole or who suggest that religion, by its nature, is a source of conflict.

It is wrong to use religion as a cover for political, economic or ideological causes. It compounds the wrong when extremists of any religious tradition radically distort their professed faith in order to justify violence and hatred. Whatever the motivation, there can be no religious or moral justification for what happened on September 11. People of all faiths must be united in the conviction that terrorism in the name of religion profanes religion. The most effective counter to terrorist claims of religious justification comes from within the world's rich religious traditions and from the witness of so many people of faith who have been a powerful force for non-violent human liberation around the world.

A deeper appreciation of the role that religion plays in world affairs is needed, as is a deeper understanding of and engagement with Islam. The Catholic community is engaged in dialogue and common projects with Muslims at many levels and in many ways in this country and around the world. To cite just one example, in many countries Catholic Relief Services is involved in fruitful collaboration with Muslim organizations committed to peace, justice and human rights. More should be done at all levels to deepen and broaden this dialogue and common action.

The duty to preserve the common good, protect the innocent, and reestablish peace and order

Our nation, in collaboration with other nations and organizations, has a moral right and a grave obligation to defend the common good against mass terrorism. The common good is threatened when innocent people are targeted by terrorists. Therefore, we support efforts of our nation and the international community to seek out and hold accountable, in accord with national and international law, those individuals, groups and governments which are responsible. How the common good is defended and peace is restored is a critical moral issue. While military action may be necessary, it is by no means sufficient to deal with this terrorist threat. From bolstering homeland security and ensuring greater transparency of the financial system to strengthening global cooperation against terrorism, a wide range of non-military measures must be pursued. Among these measures is a persistent effort to pursue negotiations that would work to protect the interests of both Afghanistan and the United States

Considerable sacrifice by all will be needed if this broad-based, long-term effort in defense of the common good is to succeed. We must never lose sight, however, of the basic ideals of justice, freedom, fairness, and openness that are hallmarks of our society. We must not trade freedom for security. We must not allow ourselves to be captured by fear. Acts of ethnic and religious intolerance towards Arab-Americans, Muslims, or any other minorities must be repudiated. It is the glory of our nation that out of many, we are one.

As criminal and civil investigations proceed and essential security measures are strengthened, our government must continue to respect the basic rights of all persons and in a special way of immigrants and refugees. Care must be taken to avoid assigning collective guilt to all newcomers or undermine our history as a land of immigrants and a safe haven for the world's persecuted. The United States must not shrink from its global leadership role in offering protection to refugees who flee terror in their homelands. Proposals to ensure the security of our legal immigration system and refugee program must avoid harming immigrants and refugees who represent no security threat. Enforcement actions must not be indiscriminate in their application or based upon ethnic background, national origin, or religious affiliation. The suspension of refugee admissions is particularly inappropriate.

Conclusion

It has been said many times that September 11 changed the world. That is true in many ways, but the essential tasks of our community of faith continue with a new urgency and focus. The weeks and months and years ahead will be:

A time for prayer. We pray for the victims and their families; for our president and national leaders; for police and fire fighters; postal, health care and relief workers; and for military men and women. We pray for an end to terror and violence. We also pray for the Afghan people and for our adversaries. We call on Catholics to join in a National Day of Prayer for Peace on January 1, 2002.

A time for fasting. As long as this struggle continues, we urge Catholics to fast one day a week. This fast is a sacrifice for justice, peace and for the protection of innocent human life.

A time for teaching. Many Catholics know the Church's teaching on war and peace. Many do not. This is a time to share our principles and values, to invite discussion and continuing dialogue within our Catholic community. Catholic universities and colleges, schools and parishes should seek opportunities to share the Sacred Scripture and Church teaching on human life, justice and peace more broadly and completely. In a special way we should seek to help our children feel secure and safe in these difficult days.

A time for dialogue. This is a time to engage in dialogue with Muslims, Jews, fellow Christians and other faith communities. We need to know more about and understand better other faiths, especially Islam. We also need to support our interfaith partners in clearly repudiating terrorism and violence, whatever its source. (See Joint Statement of Catholic Bishops and Muslim Leaders, September 14, 2001). As the Holy Father recently said, dialogue is essential for ensuring that "the name of the one God becomes increasingly what it is: a name for peace and a summons to peace." (Remarks to Pope John Paul II Cultural Center, November 6, 2001).

A time for witness. In our work and communities, we should live our values of mutual respect, human dignity and respect for life. We should seek security without embracing discrimination. We should use our voices to protect human life, to seek greater justice, and to pursue peace as participants in a powerful democracy.

A time for service. Catholic Charities throughout the United States is providing assistance to families, parishes, neighborhoods and communities directly affected by the attacks on September 11. Catholic hospitals in these cities are also in the forefront in caring for those injured in these attacks. Catholic Relief Services is providing critical aid to Afghan refugees and doing invaluable work throughout Central Asia and the Middle East. This is a time for generous and sacrificial giving.

American Catholic servicemen and women and their chaplains are likewise called conscientiously to fulfill their duty to defend the common good. To risk their own lives in this defense is a great service to our nation and an act of Christian virtue.

A time for solidarity. We are not the first to experience such horrors. We now understand better the daily lot of millions around the world who have long lived under the threat of violence and uncertainty and have refused to give in to fear or despair. As we stand in solidarity with the victims of the terrorist attacks and their families, we must also stand with those who are suffering in Afghanistan. We stand with all those whose lives are at risk and whose dignity is denied in this dangerous world.

A time for hope. Above all, we need to turn to God and to one another in hope. Hope assures us that, with God's grace, we will see our way through what now seems such a daunting challenge. For believers, hope is not a matter of optimism, but a source for strength and action in demanding times. For peacemakers, hope is the indispensable virtue. This hope, together with our response to the call to conversion, must be rooted in God's promise and nourished by prayer, penance, and acts of charity and solidarity.

Our nation and the Church are being tested in fundamental ways. Our nation has a right and duty to respond and must do so in right ways, seeking to defend the common good and build a more just and peaceful world. Our community of faith has the responsibility to live out in our time the challenges of Jesus in the Beatitudes — to comfort those who mourn, to seek justice, to become peacemakers. We face these tasks with faith and hope, asking God to protect and guide us as we seek to live out the Gospel of Jesus Christ in these days of trial.

25
A New Evangelization

Pope John Paul II has issued a clarion call for every Christian and person of good will to stand up and be counted. That is our God-given privilege and responsibility. He has stated clearly that Christ's words, "You too go," are addressed to every person of good will. We must be willing to make the difference by being willing to pay the price through personal involvement. We must be willing to risk everything, to raise high the flag of right living.

1. Pray
First and foremost, we must pray that God will give us the wisdom and the courage to understand His plan. Pray that God will change or remove Godless men and women from positions of leadership, not only in politics but also in the legal, medical and entertainment professions. Pray that the media will assume its rightful role to be an ambassador of good news rather than of bad news. Pray that God will provide healing for our families, our schools, our children and our institutions. Pray that God will give each one of us the courage to make our own lives an example of obedience to His Spirit. Pray that we will keep our minds and hearts set upon the goal — one country under God once again, a nation that reflects God's principles in our homes, in our schools, in our marriages, in our parishes, in our newspapers, in our movies, in our courts.

2. Become Informed
Just as an untrained soldier is at the mercy of his enemy, the uninformed evangelist is incapable of prevailing against the forces

of evil in the world of politics. In order to serve God and country, we must learn how to use the existing political processes for God's work. It would be wise that each one of us would pick out a specific area. For example, the reform of our schools, or the reform of our media, or the reform of our families, or the reform of our youth. Be willing to study Christian magazines and journals. Be willing to go to the public library and read about your growing area of interest. Be willing to write letters and make use of public access on your local cable television stations. Be willing to meet with your local politicians, your state board of education. Be willing to communicate with other like-minded people about your area of concern. Be willing to communicate with elected representatives.

3. Register to Vote

Although this is such a simple process, many do not register and, if they do register, a vast majority do not vote. We saw how the last presidential election was decided by the tiniest of margins.

4. Attend Your Political Party's Precinct and Political Meetings

At these meetings, people are selected as delegates for county and state meetings. In most states, the county and state meetings will adopt a platform. In some states they will elect delegates to national conventions. Get involved and be part of the process.

5. Seek Out and Support Men and Women of Integrity

Encourage people of integrity to get involved in the political process. When Christians fail to influence the political process, the society is left to flounder unprotected against the forces of evil. You can hold a home meeting for potential candidates and invite members of your parish to attend. You can write a letter on their behalf or start up a phone campaign. You can get others to contribute money to their campaign.

6. Help Your Pastor to Inform Church Members

Collecting important dates for voter registration, elections, political meetings, dates of public hearings is vitally important for

Christian citizens. One of your major contributions can be keeping your fellow parishioners and pastor well informed on what they can do.

7. Contribution of Time, Talent and Treasure

Every successful campaign needs many volunteers to donate time, energy and financial assistance. Advertisements will be necessary, as well as printing, office facilities, postage, telephones, meeting halls. Be willing to sacrifice yourself.

8. Letter-Writing

Be willing to write to your senator, to your representative, to your mayor, to your school board and to your political party officers. Be willing to give praise where praise is merited, and gentle correction where it is due. Make sure you know your subject and be specific. In general, stay away from form letters and ask for a reply. Write often and pray much. As Everett Hale stated, "I am only one, but I am one. I cannot do everything, but I can do something. What I can do, I should do; and, with the help of God, I will do."

Pope John Paul II
Pope John Paul II's Call to America
Be Renewed by the Gospel

During his last visit to the United States, Pope John Paul II challenged each of us to work to fulfill the destiny of our nation by fidelity to America's founding principles and through faithful witness to our Christian faith. Highlights of the Holy Father's addresses are excerpted below.

Newark Airport, October 4
One From Many

. . . From its beginning until now, the United States has been a haven for generation after generation of new arrivals. Men, women and children have streamed here from every corner of the globe, building new lives and forming a society of rich ethnic and racial diversity, based on commitment to a shared vision of human dignity and freedom. Of the United States we can truly say, *E pluribus Unum.*

It is my prayerful hope that America will persevere in its own best traditions of openness and opportunity. It would indeed be sad if the United States were to turn away from that enterprising spirit, which has always sought the most practical and responsible ways of continuing to share with others the blessings God has richly bestowed here.

Spirit of Creative Generosity

The same spirit of creative generosity will help you to meet the needs of your own poor and disadvantaged. They, too, have a role to play in building a society truly worthy of the human person — a society in which none are so poor that they have nothing to give and none are so rich that they have nothing to receive. The poor have needs which are not only material and economic, but also involve liberating their potential to work out their own destiny and to provide for the well being of their families and communities. America will continue to be a land of promise as long as it remains a land of freedom and justice for all. . .

Giants Stadium East Rutherford, N.J., October 5
Church in America Has Found a Home

Tonight we give thanks to God for the way in which the Church has "made a home" in America. From the beginning in this new land, the Church grew out of the faith of peoples from many cultural and ethnic backgrounds, embracing the indigenous people and settlers alike. Everywhere, we see the results of the labors of countless priests, religious sisters and brothers, Christian families and individual lay men and women who made the Church present in American society through a great network of parishes, schools, hospitals and charitable institutions. This proud heritage should serve as an inspiration and an incentive for you as you seek to meet the challenges of our own times.

No Prejudices Allowed

To a great extent, the story of America has been the story of long and difficult struggles to overcome the prejudices which excluded certain categories of people from a full share in the country's life: first, the struggle against religious intolerance, then the struggle against racial discrimination and in favor of civil rights for everyone.

Baby — Stranger in the Womb

Sadly, today a new class of people is being excluded. When the unborn child — the "stranger in the womb" — is declared to be beyond the protection of society, not only are America's deepest traditions radically undermined and endangered, but a moral blight is brought upon society. I am also thinking of threats to the elderly, the severely handicapped and all those who do not seem to have any social usefulness. When innocent human beings are declared inconvenient or burdensome, and thus unworthy of legal and social protection, grievous damage is done to the moral foundations of the democratic community.

Right to Life

The right to life is the first of all rights. It is the foundation of democratic liberties and the keystone of the edifice of civil society. Both as Americans and as followers of Christ, American Catholics must be committed to the defense of life in all its stages and in every condition. . .

True Value of Our Culture

Our confidence in the future which God has opened before us enables us to see this earthly life in its proper light. In the perspective of God's kingdom, we discern the true value of all the accomplishments of human civilization and culture, of all our achievements, our struggles and our sufferings. As Americans, you are rightly proud of your country's great achievements. As Christians, you know that all things human are the soil in which the kingdom of God is meant to take root and mature! To the Church in the United States, I make this appeal: Do not make an idol of any temporal reality! "Know that the kingdom of God is at hand" (cf. Lk 10:11). "Wait for the Lord with courage; be stouthearted" (Ps 27:14). Hope in the Lord! Amen.

Aqueduct Racetrack, Queens, N.Y. October 6
Family is Sacred
...Society must strongly reaffirm the right of the child to grow up in a family in which, as far as possible, both parents are present. Fathers of families must accept their full share of responsibility for the lives and upbringing of their children. Both parents must spend time with their children and be personally interested in their moral and religious education. Children need not only material support from their parents but, more important, a secure, affectionate and morally correct family environment.

Catholic Parents
Catholic parents must learn to form their family as a "domestic church," a church in the home as it were, where God is honored, his law is respected, prayer is a normal event, virtue is transmitted by word and example, and everyone shares the hopes, the problems and sufferings of everyone else. All this is not to advocate a return to some outdated style of living: It is to return to the roots of human development and human happiness!

St. Joseph's Seminary, Dunwoodie, (Yonkers) N.Y., October 6
True Wisdom form God
...Even some who call themselves Christians do not recognize that Christ is the eternal Son of the Father who brings true wisdom into the world. For this reason, they do not understand or accept the teachings of the Church. Perhaps you have already been confronted by this. You will certainly have to confront it as priests. If you are to become priests, it will be for the purpose - above all other purposes - of proclaiming the Word of God and feeding God's people with the Body and Blood of Christ. If you do this faithfully, teaching the wisdom that comes from above, you will often be ignored as Christ was ignored, and even rejected as Christ was rejected. "I preach Christ and Christ crucified," says St. Paul (cf. 1 Cor. 1:23).

Opposition to Christ

Why has the Pope come to Dunwoodie to give you such a serious message? Because in Christ we are friends (cf. Jn 15:15), and friends can talk about serious matters. If there is one challenge facing the Church and her priests today, it is the challenge of transmitting the Christian message whole and entire, without letting it be emptied of its substance. The Gospel cannot be reduced to mere human wisdom. Salvation lies not in clever human words or schemes, but in the cross and resurrection of our Lord Jesus Christ. The wisdom of the cross is at the heart of the life and ministry of every priest. This is the sublime "science" which, above all other learning, the seminary is meant to impart to you: "The Spirit we have received is not the world's spirit but God's Spirit . . . We speak . . . not in words of human wisdom, but in words taught by the Spirit" (1 Cor 2:12-13).

Courage to Follow Christ

. . .You need courage to follow Christ, especially when you recognize that so much of our dominant culture is a culture of flight from God, a culture which displays a not-so-hidden contempt for human life, beginning with the lives of the unborn and extending to contempt for the frail and the elderly. Some people say that the Pope speaks too much about the "culture of death." But these are times in which — as I wrote in my encyclical *Evangelium Vitae* - "choices once unanimously considered criminal and rejected by the common moral sense are gradually becoming socially acceptable" (no. 4). The Church cannot ignore what is happening. . .

Central Park, New York City, October 7
Like Mary - Be Not Afraid

. . .Like Mary, you must not be afraid to allow the Holy Spirit to help you become intimate friends of Christ. Like Mary, you must put aside any fear, in order to take Christ to the world in whatever you do — in marriage, as single people in the world, as students, as workers, as professional people. Christ wants to go to many places in the world and to enter many hearts through you. Just as Mary visited Elizabeth, so you too are called to "visit" the needs of the poor, the hungry, the homeless, those who are alone or ill, for example those suffering form AIDS. You are called to stand up for life! To respect and defend the mystery of life always and everywhere, including the lives of unborn babies, giving real help and encouragement to mothers in difficult situations.

Stand Up for the Poor

You are called to work and pray against abortion, against violence of all kinds, including the violence done against women's and children's dignity through pornography. Stand up for the life of the aged and the handicapped, against attempts to promote assisted suicide and euthanasia! Stand up for marriage and family life! Stand up for purity! Resist the pressures and temptations of a world that too often tries to ignore a most fundamental truth: that every life is a gift form God our Creator, and that we must give an account to God of how we use it either for good or evil. . .

St. Patrick's Cathedral, New York, October 7
Difficult Time

. . .From many points of view, these are difficult times for parents who wish to pass on to their children the treasure of the Catholic faith. Sometimes you yourselves are not sure what the Church stands for. There are false teachers and dissenting voices. Bad examples cause great harm. Furthermore, a self-indulgent culture undermines many of the values which are at the basis of sound family life.

There are two immediate things which the Catholic families of America can do to strengthen home life. The first is prayer: both personal and family prayer. Prayer raises our minds and hearts to God to thank Him for his blessings, to ask Him for his help. It brings the saving power of Jesus Christ into the decisions and actions of everyday life.

Pray the Rosary

One prayer, in particular, I recommend to families: the one we have just been praying, the Rosary. And especially the joyful mysteries, which help us to meditate on the Holy Family of Nazareth.

Uniting her will with the will of God, Mary conceived the Christ Child and became the model of every mother carrying her unborn child. By visiting her cousin, Elizabeth, Mary took to another family the healing presence of Jesus. Mary gave birth to the infant Jesus in the humblest of circumstances and presented Him to Simeon in the temple, as every baby may be presented to God in Baptism. Mary and Joseph worried over the lost Child before they found Him in the Temple, so that parents of all generations would know that the trials and sorrows of family life are the road to closer union with Jesus. To use a phrase made famous by the late Fr. Patrick Peyton: The family that prays together, stays together!

Use the New Catechism
The second suggestion I make to families is to use the Catechism of the Catholic Church to learn about the faith and to answer the questions that come up, especially the moral questions which confront everyone today.

Dear parents, you are educators because you are parents. I exhort and encourage the bishops and the whole Church in the United States to help parents to fulfill their vocation to be the first and most important teachers of the faith to their children. . .

Camden Yards, Baltimore, October 8
Be a Witness
. . .Christian witness takes different forms at different moments in the life of a nation. Sometimes, witnessing to Christ will mean drawing out of a culture the full meaning of its noblest intentions, a fullness that is revealed in Christ. At other times, witnessing to Christ means challenging that culture, especially when the truth about the human person is under assault. America has always wanted to be a land of the free. Today, the challenge facing America is to find freedom's fulfillment in the truth: the truth that is intrinsic to human life created in God's image and likeness, the truth that is written on the human heart, the truth that can be known by reason and can therefore form the basis of a profound and universal dialogue among people about the direction they must give to their lives and their activities.

Fulfill Lincoln's Dream

One hundred thirty years ago, President Abraham Lincoln asked whether a nation "conceived in liberty and dedicated to the proposition that all men are created equal" could "long endure." President Lincoln's question is no less a question for the present generation of Americans. Democracy cannot be sustained without a shared commitment to certain moral truths about the human person and human community. The basic question before a democratic society is, "How ought we to live together?" In seeking an answer to this question, can society exclude moral truth and moral reasoning? Can the biblical wisdom which played such a formative part in the very founding of your country be excluded from that debate? Would not doing so mean that America's founding documents no longer have any defining content, but are only the formal dressing of changing opinion? Would not doing so mean that tens of millions of Americans could no longer offer the contribution of their deepest convictions to the formation of public policy? Surely it is important for America that the moral truths which make freedom possible should be passed on to each new generation. Every generation of Americans needs to know that freedom consists not in doing what we like, but in having the right to do what we ought . . .

BWI Airport, Baltimore, October 8
A Model and Pattern.

. . .I express to the Catholic community of the United States my heartfelt thanks! In the words of St. Paul: "I give thanks to my God every time I think of you — which is constantly in every prayer I utter" (Phil 1:3).

I say this, too, to the United States of America: Today, in our world as it is, many other nations and peoples look to you as the principal model and pattern for their own advancement in democracy. But democracy needs wisdom. Democracy needs virtue, if it is not to turn against everything that it is meant to defend and encourage. Democracy stands or falls with the truths and values which it embodies and promotes.

Good Democracy

Democracy serves what is true and right when it safeguards the dignity of every human person, when it respects inviolable and inalienable human rights, when it makes the common good the end and criterion regulating all public and social life. But these values themselves must have an objective content. Otherwise they correspond only to the power of the majority or the wishes of the most vocal. If an attitude of skepticism were to succeed in calling into question even the fundamental principles of the moral law, the democratic system itself would be shaken in its foundations (cf. *Evangelium Vitae*, no. 70).

Declaration of Independence

The United States possesses a safeguard, a great bulwark, against this happening. I speak of your founding documents: the Declaration of Independence, the Constitution, the Bill of Rights. These documents are grounded in and embody unchanging principles of the natural law whose permanent truth and validity can be known by reason, for it is the law written by God in human hearts (cf. Rom 2:25).

At the center of the moral vision of your founding documents is the recognition of the rights of the human person, and especially respect for the dignity and sanctity of human life in all conditions and at all stages of development. I say to you again, America, in the light of your own tradition: Love life, cherish life, defend life, from conception to natural death. . .

Be Revealed by the Gospel

Vatican City, October 18, the Holy Father reflected positively on his American visit and emphasized the importance of American renewal.

Like every nation, America must be renewed by the power of the Gospel!. . .

But how can we forget that a democratic nation "Stands or falls with the truths and values which it embodies and promotes" (BWI Airport, Oct. 8)? These values are not determined by majority vote or the desires of those who shout the loudest, but by the principles of the law written by God in the human heart. . .

26
Prayer Strategies for Changing America and Our World

Thank and praise God for who He is and for the privilege of cooperating with Him in the exciting ministry of changing the world. That is why Jesus came as its Light. Then thank Him for what He's already done in the nations.

Pray for an unprecedented outpouring of the Holy Spirit in revival power to come upon God's people.

Pray for God to unite the Body of Christ and the family of man: Catholics with Protestants, Christians with Moslems, blacks with whites, young with the old, men with women, believers with nonbelievers.

We need to humble ourselves before God and acknowledge that the body of Christ in our nation has sinned. We have allowed materialism, promiscuity, violence, and disobedience to overwhelm our land.

Try to attend daily Mass, pray the Rosary and make Eucharistic Holy Hours.

Pray for leaders that they may follow the inspirations of the Spirit.

Be willing to fast on Fridays.

Pray that terrorists may be brought to justice as swiftly as possible with a very minimum of violence.

Never allow hatred, bitterness or violence to permeate your heart. We are to overcome hatred with love and violence with forgiveness and peace.

Pray that the Word of God, once again, will be given its rightful place as the basis for the formation of just laws, and as the standard for moral values and behavior.

Unite to make this nation "a nation under God" once again.

Meditate upon Scripture and the New Catechism each day. They are God's love letters to His people.

Teach our children that we need religion and morality to be the twin pillars upon which this nation was built. Let them know that America has been under attack since 1962 when our Supreme Court took God away from our public schools; and since 1973 when our Supreme Court no longer upheld the God-given, self-evident, inalienable right to life of every American citizen, including the unborn.

Pray that God will change the movies, the music and the media that have been filling our minds and the minds of our children with so much violence, promiscuity and paganism.

Pray that God will send laborers into the fields to form apostolates and circles of prayer.

Ask God to stir spiritual leaders to teach people about the need to help the poor and needy.

Pray for great spiritual awakening to come upon the unconverted, motivating them to seek God.

Ask God to name the major principalities over the nations and cities and wage spiritual warfare as directed by the Holy Spirit.

Finish by praising God, declaring faith in His promise to restore our nation and heal our land.

Keep on persisting in intercession. Don't let up. God will be faithful if we are faithful.

27
A Prayer for America

Heavenly Father,

At Fatima, You sent us the Mother of Your Son to call us back to Him and to warn us of the rise of Communism and a second World War more terrible than the first. By and large, we did not listen. We did not pray and fast, and were not converted. And so You allowed three Christian European countries — Russia, Germany and Italy — to reject You and the sanctity of human life; and as a result, over 150 million people were killed.

Then, in our own country, we did the unthinkable. In 1962, we publicly declared that we were no longer a nation under You and would not allow our public officials or school children to pray. Then in 1973, we turned against the sanctity of human life and allowed abortion on demand. We no longer held these truths to be self evident that all men and all women - including the unborn - were endowed by their Creator with certain inalienable rights, first and foremost, the right to life.

Pornography has become mainstream America. Our TV programs, magazines and songs have become revolting. Our comedians mock You and our plays desecrate Your name. Our marriages are being destroyed and our youth corrupted as lust pervades our campuses.

We as a nation now repent. We come back to you in fullest faith, brightest hope, lasting love, humble repentance and gracious forgiveness. Give us the courage to truly love as You have shown us. Let us love and try to understand and to serve the young and old, black and white, Jew and Arab, Catholic and Protestant, Christian and Moslem — all of whom people our land.

May our Statue of Liberty always be an image of the Madonna of the Harbor, welcoming the poor and the homeless. May Our Lady of America, Our Lady of Guadalupe, lead us more closely to Jesus to help us, like her, to listen to the Father, love with the Son and live with the Spirit. May we forever sing,

Let the storm clouds gather, far across the sea.
Let us pledge allegiance to a land that is free.
Let us all be faithful to a land so fair,
As we raise our voices in a solemn prayer.

God Bless America,
Land that I love,
Stand beside her and guide her
Through the night, with a Light from above.

From the mountains, to the prairies,
to the oceans white with foam,
God Bless America, My home sweet home.

God Bless America, My home sweet home. Amen.

Epilogue

Without Me

It is a basic Christian dictum that without Christ we cannot have a great America. His grace perfects, heals and elevates us. Conversely left to our own devices we dehumanize, hurt, destroy, use and paganize each other. Whether liberal Americans want to believe it or not, Christ can never be accidental to the American dream. He is too much a part of it. He is the best of that dream. Our laws and constitution are founded upon His Gospel. His Gospel introduced justice, love, and liberty to our land. We were pro-God, pro-family, pro-life, pro-decency because of Him. This is our history - HIS-STORY.

Take Him Out

In so far as we have taken His influence from us, we have become degenerate. Our children are paying the price. Virtually two generations never knew *A Nation Under God;* never learned the Ten Commandments in school. Therefore, they never thought of them as truly American. Turn on their music, go to their concerts, listen to their comedians, see their movies, read their magazines, visit their dorms and come away shocked. The deeper question is how can we, their elders, condone and accept such widespread child abuse. The vulgarization and paganization of our youth is not a peripheral problem. It strikes at the root of who we are. If all this continues for another generation or two the great American experiment will be over. Our nation will decay from within. The real terrorists are striking at the twin towers of religion and morality.

Power of the Spirit

The Spirit of Christ can transform us if we sign, cry and pray for it to come to renew us. The Spirit of '76 is the Spirit of Christ. Those who do not know our history will fail to recognize this great truth. This county was founded, established by Christians, and upon the Gospel of Jesus. That is precisely why Heaven so blessed us. It wasn't our genius, our work, our fortitude that made us great. It was our faith - the faith of our fathers. Throw away the Spirit of '76 and you throw away the soul of America. Relativize it and you neutralize it. Fan it into a flame once more and it will transform us. His Spirit alone does transform us. In the light of the political shift of the 2002 Mid-term elections we can expect more and more discussions about moral issues. The issues of pornography, abortion, promiscuity, co-ed dorms, euthanasia, public deceit, corporate dishonesty, clergy abuse, poverty, violence and war, homelessness, the gap between first and third worlds won't go away. They continually haunt us until we correct them. Like it or not both civilization and culture, as well as God and religion, demand this. Every civilization that does not right its wrongs will perish. God Himself will see to it. If however we repent and turn from our wicked ways - "He will heal our nation and restore our land."

God's Plan in Summary Form (15 Principles)

1. Let God be God

This is the first and the most important principle. Let God be God. God is the Supreme Master of the Universe. He is the potter, we are the clay. He is the Creator, we are the creatures. He the Vine, we are the branches. He is the Son, we live in the Sonlight. He is the Ocean, we live in His waters. *In Him we live and move and have our being.* So let God have His way.

We do this by surrender. Let go of your plans, be open to HIS plan. Let go of your petty insights, be open to HIS Wisdom. Let go of your vested interests, be open to HIS love. Let go of the small, be open to the large. Let go of the denominational, be open to the universal (Catholic). Let go of division, be open to unity - for all is one in Him. He is simplicity itself, wisdom itself, holiness itself. **Let go and let God. Let God be God.** You and I are not God. This is such a simple truth; but because of the sin of Adam and Eve, most people do not really believe it. We are perverted humanists, secularists, practical pagans. We give God at times lip service, but not our minds, our wills or our hearts. We seek freedom from His restraint, His will, His plans. This brings all the sufferings, sins and evils of he world. So please, let *God Be God!*

2. Let You Be His

Since He is the source of everything, consecrate yourself to Him often. Consecrate your mind and your heart, your will and your emotions, your time and your talent, your friends and your foes, your past and your future, your whole self and your life. Be willing to live a life of poverty, chastity and obedience. By making Jesus your treasure, you can be poor in spirit. By making Jesus your romance, you can be pure. By making Jesus your Lord, you can be obedient. Say this simple prayer:

> *Dear Jesus, to You I consecrate my mind* (—make the sign of the cross on your cross on your forehead). *My heart* (— make the sign of the cross on your heart), *my lips* (—make the sign of the cross on your lips). *My entire self* (—make the sign of the cross on each shoulder). *I am yours. Amen.*

3. Let God's Will Be Your Will.

To live in His Kingdom of the Divine Will is the greatest holiness. Next to praising and worshipping God, the highest act of holiness is to strive to listen, to discern and to obey the will of God in your life. God has a will for us, His children. He has a plan. The greatest gift we can offer is the "obedience of faith" (cf. Romans 1:6, 1:5, 16:26) - the total yes.

Jesus always did the will of His Father. This was His "food", His sustenance. Mary always did the will of God. The saints were those people who strove to do the will of God. Meditation, prayer and obedience are keys. Meditate on the person, presence and teachings of Jesus. Let them penetrate your mind and heart. Then, as Mary did, Do whatsoever He tells you. For Jesus said, "The wise man who built his house upon the rock (Christ) is he who listens to the word of the Lord and OBEYS IT!" "If you love me, obey my commands." The obedience of faith is key. In Eden. the one test, the one thing that established the sovereignty of God was obedience. Nothing was said of faith, hope, love, purity or patience. Obedience included all. The one thing that brought us back to the Tree of Life was obedience of Christ and Mary. Through the disobedience of Adam and Eve, we lost the Spirit. Through the obedience of Christ and Mary, we can regain it — if only we, like them, obey.

4. Let God's Voice Be Heard

God is speaking to all of us all of the time. He speaks externally through the covenant, the bible, the Church, creation, signs, symbols, people and events. He speaks internally through inspired thoughts, our deepest intuitions, sometimes even through dreams and visions. The most often repeated theme (over 20,000 times in the Bible) is that He speaks to us. Our prayer should often be, "Speak Lord, Your Servant is listening."

As we learn to *hear* the voice of our Shepherd, we come into His flock, His Church, His Kingdom. *The whole of the life and example of Jesus can be summed up in few words — "Yes, Abba."* Jesus always listened to, discerned and obeyed the voice of His Father (cf Jn 5:19). This is the *life more abundantly* that He promised (Jn 10:10). For Him and for us, life is a filial and obedient relationship with the source of life — that is, the Father. All life, all holiness comes from Him, through the Son, in the Spirit. To listen to, to discern, to obey the voice of God is to be alive in His Kingdom.

5. Let God's Kingdom Come

As we listen to, obey and discern the will and the voice of God, we are transplanted into a new kingdom — the realm of the Spirit where God is God and Jesus is Lord. We think thoughts inspired by His Spirit. We have desires inflamed by His love. We have lives empowered by His Spirit. Our wisdom, love and power is that of His Kingdom. We become poor in spirit, humble of heart, forgiving, loving pure, childlike and submissive as the spirit of God rules our lives. This *kingdom* we find is now *within* us. We understand all the Kingdom of God parables; for, as Jesus taught, they can only be truly understood by those who stand under Him. *He who belongs to god hears what God says* (Jn 8:47).

6. Let His Blood Cleanse

Jesus comes with a Kingdom of love and mercy. He comes to save us, to forgive us, to cleanse us of all guilt and sin as we repent and are willing to forgive those who have hurt us. He cleanses us through His Blood shed for us upon the cross.

There is great power in that blood. He has given the Church the keys to forgive and unbind. On Easter Sunday evening after His horrendous death and glorious resurrection, he appeared to his first priests, His apostles, showed them the wounds of His crucifixion, and then said, *As the Father has sent me, I now serve you. Receive the Holy Spirit. Whose sins you shall forgive, they are forgiven. Whose sins you shall retain, they are retained.* Just as in the Old Testament, it was the priest who poured the blood of the lamb upon the Mercy Seat in the holy of holies. So also, in the New testament, the blood of the lamb is administered through the priest.

Every time we go to confession, three miracles take place. First, every bit of sin and guilt is washed away. Second, all bitterness, hatred and unforgiveness is released — especially if we realize the truth of Christ's words, *Your sins are forgiven,* spoken through the priest. Third, we are given the awesome power to forgive ourselves and get on with our lives. When you realize that over 95% of all people walk around loaded with guilt, this sacrament is powerful. Most people repress guilt, deny it, rationalize it, or project it. Yet only this sacrament can cleanse and purge it. This is a powerful key that His blood cleanses.

7. Let His Body Be Eaten.

Jesus, realizing that He was calling us to a supernatural life, gave us supernatural food. He said, *With all the earnestness I possess, I tell you this, unless you feed on the flesh of he Son of man and drink His blood you have no life within you. He who eats my flesh and drinks my blood has eternal life and I will raise him up in the last day. For my flesh is real food and my blood is real drink. Whoever eats my flesh and drinks my blood has eternal life and I will raise him up on the last day. For my flesh is real food and my blood is real drink. Whoever eats my flesh and drinks my blood abides in me and I in him. Just as the Living Father sent me and I live because of Him, so the one who feeds on me will live because of me* (Jn 6:53-57).

Jesus is the bread of our life, our very sustenance. Every time we receive His body and blood at holy Mass, we become what we receive. We become bone of His bone, and flesh of His flesh, humility of His humility, love of His love. We become as bread that is broken for a darkened world. Our lives live out eucharistic celebration as we say to those we know, love and meet along the way, *this is my body, (my life), for you. This is my blood for you.*

8. Let His Church Be Revealed

The Kingdom incarnate that Christ has come to bring to earth is the one holy, apostolic, covenanted people for all men and women — that is His Church, which Jesus has left as the *pillar and standard of truth* (cf 1 Tim 3:15) Because God is one, this Church is one. Because God is holy, this Church has the means of being holy. Because God is apostolic, this Church is apostolic. And because God loves everyone, this Church is universal or Catholic. Because the God we worship is a family — that is, the Trinity of persons loving one another, deferring to one another and delighting in one another — this Church is His family upon earth (cf. *The Joy of Being Catholic*, by Fr. Bill McCarthy). Jesus said to Peter, *You are Peter and upon this rock I will build my Church.* Jesus prayed that we all may be one. *As the Father is in him and he is in the father* (cf Jn 17:20-21). And that there would be *but one flock and one shepherd* (Jn 10:167).

9. Let His Vicar — the Pope — Be Obeyed.

Since Jesus built His Church upon Peter and His successors, to whom he would give the keys of the Kingdom, we are to live in union with the pope. Knowing the weakness of human nature and our tendency toward disunity; Christ founded the new covenanted people upon one male head. In each of the previous covenants, with Adam, Noah, Abraham, Moses, Ezrah, and David, He had done the same. In Isaiah 22, David, the king of Israel, gives to his prim minister the keys to the earthly kingdom along with the authority to open doors and close doors. Using this symbolism of giving the keys of the new kingdom to a prime minister, Jesus gave the keys to Peter. Peter alone, as prime minister, and his successors are the final authority here on earth to bind and to lose. Therefore, we have to obey him in matters of faith and morals.

10. Let His Love Be Shown.

What would God's Kingdom look like if you drew a picture of it? Would it look like a bunch of monks in prayer? A room of students at a Bible school? A group of people in a court room? Or a family around a table? The last is the closest to the truth, because what God is doing upon earth is creating family His way. ***This is the covenant:*** *I will be your God and you will be my people* — which in Hebrew means family. The heart of God is that God is a family, a Trinity of persons loving one another, deferring to one another, delighting in one another, respecting one another. That is what God wants of us who He created into His *image and likeness. Let us create man (and woman) into our image and likeness so male and female God created them.* God calls us to love one another with the height, depth, length and breadth of His love. As Jesus taught, Love one another as I have loved you. We cannot do without His Spirit. When we do this, however, mankind, for the second time in history, will have discovered fire!

11. Let His Mother Be Honored

Through Jesus (the new Adam) and Mary (the new Eve), we gain our new life. We are now in the family of God, new creatures by grace. We have God as our Father and Mary as our Mother. On the cross, Jesus gave Mary to John and to us when he said, "Behold your mother." This is confirmed in Revelation 12:17 where it says, "Satan, angry at the woman (Mary) goes to war on the rest of her children" — that is, those who keep Gods's commandments of Jesus and bear witness to Jesus' name. *All generation shall call her blessed* (Lk 1:48). God asks us to honor our fathers and mothers. In a preeminent way, He asks us to honor Mary, His Mother, the Mother of all the living.

12. Let His Spirit Guide

God the Father and the Son have set their Spirit to enlighten our minds as we meditate and pray, to inflame our hearts as we receive the Eucharist and love, and to direct and guide our lives as we are open to the Holy Spirit. The Spirit of Christ within us wishes to guide us each and every step of the way. The Spirit will enlighten our minds as to what to do and will inflame our hearts with the desire to do it. This will guide our lives, telling us not only what to say and do, who to see, but also where not to go.

We are not alone on a minefield filled with dangers. God's Spirit is with us to warn us of all impending danger. God leads us *not into temptation, but delivers us from evil* — if we follow His directions. *My word shall be a lamp unto your feet.* He will guide every step of our journey lest we stray into sin and danger. The Spirit brings the gifts of wisdom and understanding, compassion and forgiveness, healing and power. The fruits of the Spirit's presence will be *love, joy, peace, patience, gentleness, kindness and self control* (cf Gal. 5:22). So I *say live by the Spirit* (Gal 5:16).

13. Let His Fire Start.

Jesus said, *I have come to bring fire on the earth, and now I wish it were already enkindled* (Lk 12:45). We sing, *Come Holy Spirit, Let the Fire Fall, and Fire, Fire, Fire... Fire fell on me; as the day of Pentecost, fire fell on me.* The Spirit's coming on Pentecost was accompanied by flames of fire. The Spirit of God wants to fire us up, to excite us, to set our hearts aglow. We are to lethargic, too lukewarm, too lazy, too laid back. There is an urgency in the things of God. *Those who wait upon the Lord shall renew their strength, they shall rid as if on wings of eagles. They shall run but not grow weary. They shall walk but not grow weak* (Is 40:31).

When we ride the new wind of the Spirit, our lives will be inspired, our minds will be enlightened and our hearts will be on fire. We will understand what the disciples on the road to Emmaus meant when they said, *Were not our hearts burning inside us, as He walked with us along the way* (Lk 4:32). Our prayer will be, *Come Holy spirit, fill the hearts of the faithful and enkindle within us the fire of your love.*

14. Let His Mission Unfold.

Once we are fired up Christians, we will spread the fire. We shall discover the truth of the evangelization maxim: *If you attract a crowd, set yourself on fire.* People are attracted to inspired people whose faces are radiant with the love of Christ. The love of Christ will impel us to spread His Gospel. His great commision — *To make disciples of all nations...to spread His kingdom...to be His witness* — will be our command. The love of Christ, burning inside us, will become diffusive of itself. And the fire will spread. The kingdom will expand, and more and more men and women will be brought to Christ. They will be saved and healed and inspired themselves.

15. Let God Have the Glory

Once we, like mirrors, reflect the fire of God's love, once we become the light of the world, men and women will give glory to God. *To God be the Glory*, as the hymn sings. *Not to us, O Lord, not to us, but to your name give the glory,* the psalmist admonished.

We are here on earth to give glory to God. Whether we eat or drink, we do it to glorify the Lord. We will spend our eternity saying, *Holy, Holy, Holy is the Lord God of Hosts.* We are surrounded, even now, by a heavenly chorus of saints and angels giving all the glory, the honor, the adoration and the praise to God.

Let God have the glory!

If there is righteousness in the heart, there will be beauty in the character.
If there be beauty in the character, there will be harmony at home.
If there is harmony in the home, there will be order in the nation.
When there is order in the nation, there will be peace in the world.
—Anonymous